THE CHILDREN'S PICTORIAL
ATLAS
OF THE WORLD

THE CHILDREN'S PICTORIAL
ATLAS
OF THE WORLD

Alison Cooper
Anne McRae

Illustrated by
Daniela De Luca

BARRON'S EDUCATIONAL SERIES, INC.

First edition for the United States and Canada, published 1998 by Barron's Educational Series, Inc.

Copyright © McRae Books 1998
Via dei Rustici, 5–Florence, Italy

All inquiries should be addressed to:
Barron's Educational Series, Inc.
250 Wireless Boulevard
Hauppauge, New York 11788
http://www.barronseduc.com

Library of Congress Catalog Card No. 98–72686
International Standard Book No. 0–7641–5062–6

Text: Alison Cooper and Anne McRae
Illustrations: Daniela De Luca
Additional Illustrations: Paola Holguín
Picture Research: Antonella Meucci

Design: Marco Nardi
Editing: Anne McRae and Cath Senker

Printed in Italy by Giunti Industrie Grafiche (Prato, Italy)

Contents

Planet Earth

The earth is a planet in the solar system, orbiting around the sun. Millions of years ago, the solar system was a gigantic cloud of hot gases and particles. Gradually clouds of material joined together to form the sun and the planets. The way the earth moves in relation to the sun affects the seasons and the climate. The way it spins on its axis creates day and night.

North and south

An imaginary horizontal line around the center of the earth called the equator, divides the planet into the northern hemisphere and the southern hemisphere. The most northerly point of the northern hemisphere is called the North Pole. The South Pole is the most southerly point of the southern hemisphere.

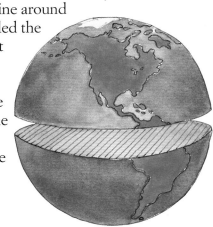

NORTH AND SOUTH

The solar system

The solar system is a group of nine planets that orbit the sun. It takes approximately 365 days for the earth to orbit the sun. The moon is a satellite of the earth. It orbits the earth every 29.5 days. Some planets have more than one moon – Jupiter has at least thirteen.

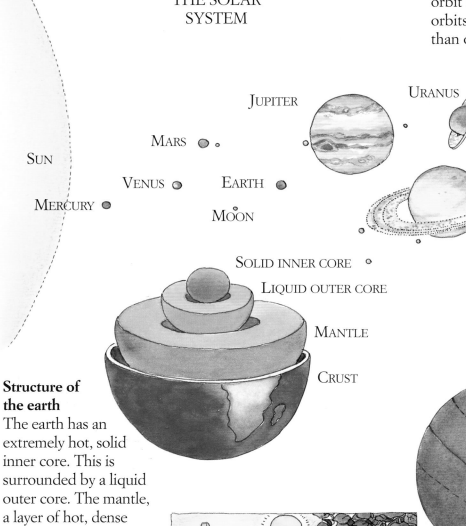

THE SOLAR SYSTEM

SUN
MERCURY
VENUS
MARS
EARTH
MOON
JUPITER
URANUS
NEPTUNE
PLUTO
SATURN

SOLID INNER CORE
LIQUID OUTER CORE
MANTLE
CRUST

Structure of the earth

The earth has an extremely hot, solid inner core. This is surrounded by a liquid outer core. The mantle, a layer of hot, dense rock, lies over the core. The earth's top layer is called the crust. It is the thinnest layer, measuring about 40–45 miles thick under the mountain ranges, but just 4 miles thick under parts of the ocean floor.

Summer

SUMMER IN THE NORTH

WINTER IN THE SOUTH

Summer in the northern hemisphere

Now the northern hemisphere is tilted towards the sun. It is summer in the north. It is winter in the south.

DAY AND NIGHT

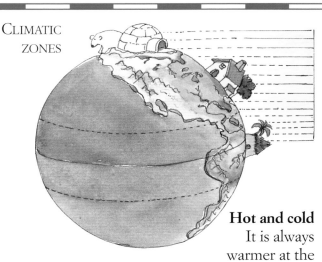

CLIMATIC ZONES

Day and night
The earth makes a complete rotation on its axis every 24 hours. It is daytime in the half that is facing the sun. It is nighttime in the half that is turned away from the sun.

Hot and cold
It is always warmer at the equator than it is at the North and South Poles. This is because the earth is round. In the tropical areas near the equator the sun's rays hit the earth almost vertically, making it very hot. Moving away from the equator, the sun's rays hit the earth at a lower angle and temperatures are lower.

SPRING IN THE NORTH

FALL IN THE SOUTH

The Seasons
The earth is tilted on its axis at an angle of 23.5 degrees. As the earth moves around the sun, one hemisphere is tilted towards the sun and the other is tilted away.

SUN

SUMMER IN THE SOUTH

Spring

Winter

WINTER IN THE NORTH

Winter in the northern hemisphere
The northern hemisphere is tilted away from the sun, so it is winter there. It is summer in the southern hemisphere.

FALL IN THE NORTH

Fall

SPRING IN THE SOUTH

7

The World

The world is divided into seven continents that are further broken up into more than 190 countries.

North America

North America's highest mountain is Mount McKinley in Alaska (20,310 feet). At 280 feet below sea level, Death Valley in California is the continent's lowest point. Lake Superior, the largest and deepest of the Great Lakes, is the second-largest lake in the world. The Niagara Falls is one of the world's biggest waterfalls.

South America

The highest mountain in South America is Aconcagua in Argentina (22,835 feet). Venezuela has the world's highest waterfall, the Angel Falls. The Amazon River in Brazil is the second-longest river in the world.

Oceans and islands

The Pacific Ocean is the world's largest ocean. It covers about one-third of the earth's surface. There are about 20,000 islands in the Pacific. Greenland, in the Arctic Ocean, is the largest island.

GREENLAND
(DENMARK)

ALASKA
(USA)

ICELAND

CANADA

PACIFIC
OCEAN

UNITED
STATES OF
AMERICA

ATLANTIC
OCEAN

UNITED
KINGDOM

HOLLAN
BELGIUM

IRELAND

LUXEMBOURG
SWITZERLAND
LIECHTENSTEIN

FRANC

ANDOR

SPAIN

PORTUGAL

MEXICO

HAWAIIAN
ISLANDS

MOROCCO

ALGE

WESTERN
SAHARA

CAPE
VERDE

MAURITANIA

MALI

BAHAMAS
DOMINICAN REPUBLIC
PUERTO RICO
(USA)

CUBA

HAITI

JAMAICA

BELIZE
HONDURAS
NICARAGUA

GUATEMALA
EL SALVADOR

ANTIGUA & BARBUDA
ST. KITTS NEVIS
ST. LUCIA
BARBADOS

DOMINICA

ST. VINCENT & THE GRENADINES
GRENADA
TRINIDAD & TOBAGO

SENEGAL

GAMBIA
GUINEA-
BISSAU
SIERRA LEONE

BURKINA
FASO

GUINEA

IVORY
COAST

GHANA

COSTA RICA

PANAMA

VENEZUELA

GUYANA

FRENCH GUIANA

SURINAM

LIBERIA

TOGO

BEN

SÃO TOMÉ
& PRINCIPE

EQU
C

COLOMBIA

ECUADOR

BRAZIL

PERU

BOLIVIA

PARAGUAY

URUGUAY

CHILE

ARGENTINA

Europe
Mont Blanc in the Alps, on the border between France and Italy, is the highest mountain in Europe (15,770 feet). The Volga River in Russia is Europe's longest river, and the Caspian Sea is the world's largest lake. Russia is the biggest country in the world.

Asia
The Himalayas, which run across the border between India, China, and Nepal, are the world's highest mountains. The tallest peak of all is Mount Everest (29,030 feet). With over 1,250 million people, China has more inhabitants than any other country in the world. Japan's highest mountain is Mount Fuji (12,390 feet).

NORWAY
SWEDEN
FINLAND
ESTONIA
LATVIA
LITHUANIA
DENMARK
POLAND
BELARUS
SLOVENIA
HUNGARY
CROATIA
BOSNIA-HERZEGOVINA
YUGOSLAVIA
GERMANY
CZECH REP.
SLOVAKIA
AUSTRIA
SAN MARINO
ROMANIA
MOLDOVA
ITALY
BULGARIA
VATICAN CITY
GREECE
MALTA
ALBANIA
MACEDONIA
TUNISIA
CYPRUS
ISRAEL
SYRIA
ARMENIA
UKRAINE
GEORGIA
AZERBAIJAN
TURKEY
IRAQ
LEBANON
JORDAN
IRAN
KUWAIT
BAHRAIN
QATAR
SAUDI ARABIA
OMAN
UNITED ARAB EMIRATES
YEMEN

RUSSIA
KAZAKHSTAN
MONGOLIA
UZBEKISTAN
KYRGYZSTAN
TURKMENISTAN
TAJIKISTAN
AFGHANISTAN
PAKISTAN
CHINA
NORTH KOREA
SOUTH KOREA
JAPAN
BHUTAN
NEPAL
INDIA
BANGLADESH
MYANMAR
LAOS
MACAU
TAIWAN
THAILAND
VIETNAM
PHILIPPINES
CAMBODIA
BRUNEI
MALAYSIA
SINGAPORE
INDONESIA

PACIFIC OCEAN

PALAU
MARSHALL ISLANDS
FEDERATED STATES OF MICRONESIA
KIRIBATI
NAURU
SOLOMON ISLANDS
TUVALU
PAPUA NEW GUINEA
VANUATU
TONGA
FIJI
SAMOAN ISLANDS

LIBYA
EGYPT
NIGER
CHAD
SUDAN
ERITREA
YEMEN
DJIBOUTI
ALGERIA
CAMEROON
CENTRAL AFRICAN REPUBLIC
ETHIOPIA
SOMALIA
GABON
REPUBLIC OF CONGO
UGANDA
KENYA
RWANDA
BURUNDI
TANZANIA
MALAWI
SEYCHELLES
ANGOLA
ZAMBIA
COMOROS
MOZAMBIQUE
MADAGASCAR
MAURITIUS
ZIMBABWE
NAMIBIA
BOTSWANA
SWAZILAND
SOUTH AFRICA
LESOTHO

MALDIVES
SRI LANKA

INDIAN OCEAN

AUSTRALIA

NEW ZEALAND

Africa
The Nile River in Egypt and Sudan is the longest river in the world. Africa also has the world's biggest desert, the Sahara, which covers around 3.5 million square miles. Air temperatures here have reached 136°F, the highest ever recorded. Africa's highest mountain is Mount Kilimanjaro in Tanzania (19,340 feet).

Australasia is made up of Australia, New Zealand, and the islands in the southern Pacific Ocean. Australia is the smallest of the continents. It is also the driest, apart from Antarctica, and the flattest. The highest mountain in Australasia is Mount Cook, on New Zealand's South Island (12,310 feet).

What is a Map?

A map is a way of presenting information about a place. Many different kinds of information can be shown on a map, so it is important to use the right type of map when you are trying to find out something. If you want to know where Nigeria is, you need to look at a map of the world in an atlas. But an atlas would be no use to you if you wanted to go out for a walk. For this you would need a large-scale map that shows small features such as footpaths and houses.

Inhabitants per square mile
- Uninhabited areas
- 0–1
- 1–10
- 10–50
- 50–200
- Over 200

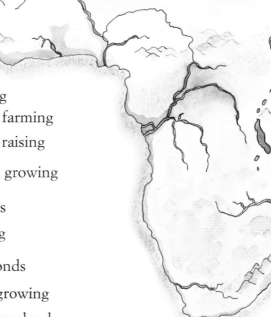

A **population map** shows how many people live in an area. These maps usually have a colored key showing the density of population in each area.

Physical maps show rivers, lakes, mountains, deserts, areas of flat land, and other physical features of the landscape. They do not usually show the borders of the countries or settlements and transportation routes. A topographic map shows both physical and man-made features.

Political maps usually show each country or region in a different color. You can use these maps to find out what part of the world a country is in and how big or small it is. Political maps sometimes show where towns and cities are too.

Economic maps show how the land is used and the main types of work that are carried out in a country or region. These maps often have picture symbols and a key to explain them.

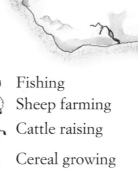

- 🐟 Fishing
- 🐑 Sheep farming
- 🐄 Cattle raising
- 🌽 Cereal growing
- 🍇 Grapes
- 🛒 Mining
- ◊ Diamonds
- Fruit growing
- Arid farmland
- Desert

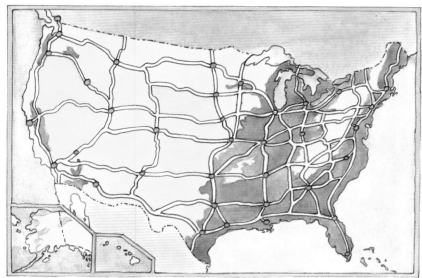

If you are planning a car journey, you need a **road map**. Road maps show the routes that link cities and towns. They usually show different types of roads in different colors, so that you can quickly tell whether a road is a country lane or an expressway.

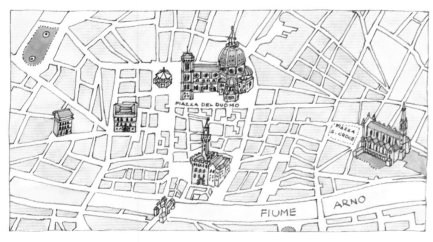

Looking at **old maps** is a good way to find out how places have changed over the centuries. New towns and roads are built and old settlements disappear. Even the shape of the coastline changes over time. Maps are much more accurate than they used to be.

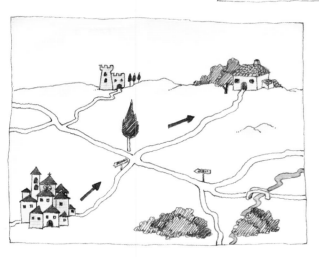

Try making a map that shows your journey to the stores or to school. Include the names of the roads and any important features, such as buildings or parks, that you pass on the way.

Bus or subway maps show the routes and how they connect with one another. They do not show the twists and turns of the roads and tunnels – the networks are simplified so it is easy to see how to get from one place to another.

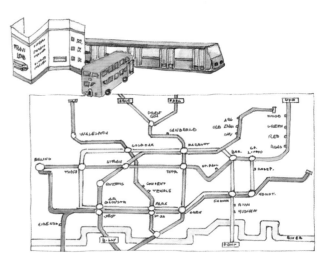

Tourist maps are large-scale maps of a region or a city. They show the road networks and usually include picture symbols showing places to visit. They can help you find places such as museums, art galleries, churches, parks, gardens, restaurants, and hotels.

Stars are divided into groups called constellations. **Star maps** show the constellations and their positions in the sky.

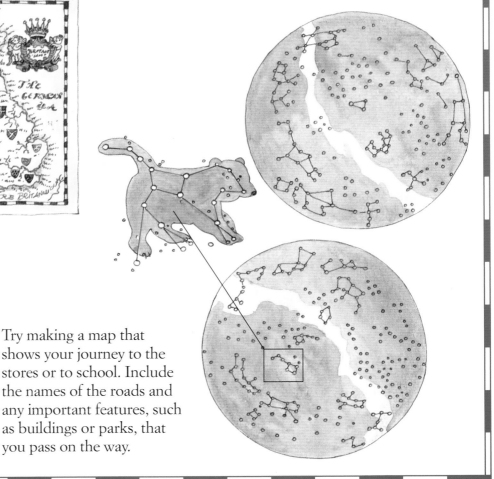

Savannas are areas of tropical grassland, with a few trees here and there. The climate is hot and quite dry. Animals that live on the savanna include elephants, giraffes, zebras, and lions.

Tropical forests are found in a broad band around the equator. Here the climate is hot and very wet. There is a rich variety of plant and animal life. Animals include monkeys, tree frogs, snakes, toucans, and parrots.

Vast **conifer forests** stretch across the northern part of the world, in Europe, Asia, and North America. Conifers thrive in cold, dry conditions. The snow slides off their sloping branches instead of breaking them with its weight. Wolves, elks, and beavers are some of the animals that live in these forests.

In areas that have mild, damp climates there are **deciduous woodlands**. Trees such as oaks, beech, and maples produce new leaves in spring and lose them each fall. Creatures that live in woodlands include foxes, deer, stoats, squirrels, owls, and woodpeckers.

Human environments are shaped by the people who live there. They cut down woodland, drain marshes, and irrigate deserts, so that they can farm the land and build settlements. They introduce new species of animals.

Deserts are very dry areas. Camels, fennec foxes, and scorpions are desert animals. Not all deserts are sandy, and they are not always hot. The Gobi Desert in China is very hot in summer, but in winter it is bitterly cold.

High in the **mountains** the air is cold, even in places where the lowlands are hot. The lower slopes are often covered in forests but near the peaks there is bare rock, or snow. Mountain animals include wild sheep and goats. Birds of prey, such as eagles, soar overhead.

Mediterranean regions have hot, dry summers and mild, wet winters. Plants tend to be low-growing shrubs such as lavender and thyme, and trees such as olives and cork oaks. They can survive with very little water in the summer months. Few large mammals live in these regions, but there are many species of insects and birds.

Many **rivers** are rich in fish in their lowland sections, just before they reach the sea. Perch, roach, and bream are common species of freshwater fish. **Lakes** are home to fish and birds such as kingfishers, herons, ducks, and grebes.

Over 70 percent of the earth's surface is covered in water. Brightly colored tropical fish dart among the coral reefs in warm ocean waters. The icy Antarctic Ocean around Antarctica is home to the blue whale, the world's largest mammal. In the very deepest parts of the oceans there are strange creatures that live in total darkness. The ocean depths are the last unexplored areas of our planet.

The world has many different environments, with different climates, landforms, plants, and animals. The map shows where the main environments are located.

World Environments

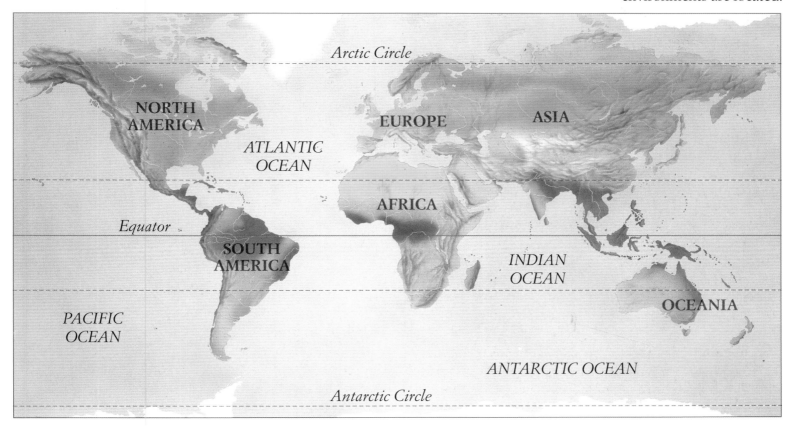

In **polar regions** temperatures are below freezing for most of the year. Polar animals have thick fur coats or layers of blubber to keep warm. Along the northern coasts of North America, Europe, and Asia lies the **tundra**. Here the snow melts briefly in summer, and lichens, mosses, and small shrubs bloom. Reindeer, arctic foxes, and snowy owls are tundra animals.

Islands often have unique species of plants and animals. This is because they have been separated from mainland species and have developed in a different way. Plant seeds and insects are carried to islands on air currents or in the water. Animals are sometimes carried to islands by passing ships.

◆ CANADA, ALASKA, AND THE ARCTIC
Canada is an independent country. Alaska is a state of the United States and Greenland is part of Denmark, although it is self-governing.

Locate the capital city of each region on the map.
1 Ottawa   **2** Nuuk (Godthab)   **3** Anchorage

The Arctic
No one lives on the drifting Arctic ice, although some people go there to hunt and explore. The North Pole is on the frozen ice.

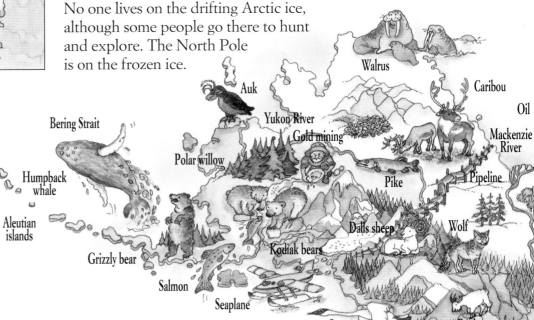

The Arctic is an ocean. Part of it is covered with drifting ice, some of which never melts. The surrounding land is covered with ice and snow all year round. Farther south, flowers bloom on the tundra during the short summer. Beyond the tundra there are great forests and plains. Canada's Great Slave Lake and Great Bear Lake are among the biggest lakes in the world. The St. Lawrence River is an important transportation route in the east.

Pipelines and pollution
The Trans-Alaska pipeline snakes across the tundra, carrying oil from the drilling sites to coastal ports. Oil is important to the economy, but there are dangers. Oil spills often cause serious damage to the environment and kill thousands of fish and sea birds.

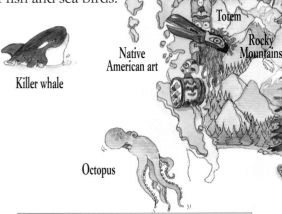

Canada, Alaska, and the Arctic

Canada is the second-biggest country in the world, but it is one of the least crowded. Very few people live in the icy Arctic regions of the north. Farther south, most people live in towns and cities. Farming, forestry, and fishing are important types of work. The main language is English but there are also many French speakers. In the Arctic, the biggest group of people are the Inuit. In the past they survived by hunting and trapping animals for their fur. Now, many work in the mining and oil drilling industries.

◆ **LOOK AT THE MAPS.**
Can you find…
• four different kinds of whale?
• the North Pole?
• two large rivers?
• three types of sport?
• the Rocky Mountains?
• Bering Strait?

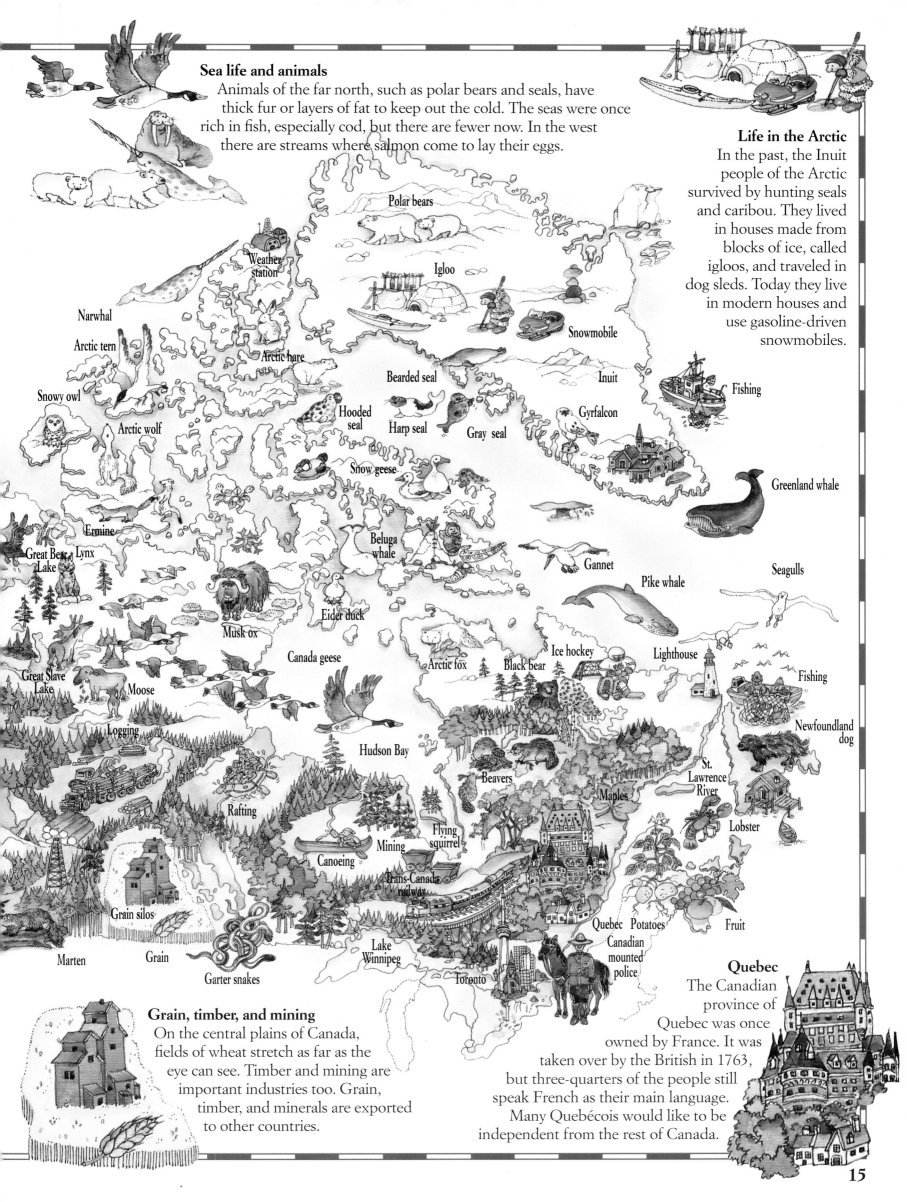

Sea life and animals
Animals of the far north, such as polar bears and seals, have thick fur or layers of fat to keep out the cold. The seas were once rich in fish, especially cod, but there are fewer now. In the west there are streams where salmon come to lay their eggs.

Life in the Arctic
In the past, the Inuit people of the Arctic survived by hunting seals and caribou. They lived in houses made from blocks of ice, called igloos, and traveled in dog sleds. Today they live in modern houses and use gasoline-driven snowmobiles.

Narwhal

Arctic tern

Snowy owl

Arctic wolf

Ermine

Great Bear Lake

Lynx

Great Slave Lake

Moose

Logging

Rafting

Canoeing

Grain silos

Marten

Grain

Garter snakes

Polar bears

Weather station

Igloo

Snowmobile

Inuit

Gyrfalcon

Bearded seal

Hooded seal

Harp seal

Gray seal

Snow geese

Beluga whale

Musk ox

Eider duck

Canada geese

Arctic fox

Black bear

Ice hockey

Hudson Bay

Beavers

Flying squirrel

Mining

Trans-Canada railway

Lake Winnipeg

Toronto

Maples

St. Lawrence River

Lobster

Fishing

Greenland whale

Seagulls

Pike whale

Gannet

Lighthouse

Fishing

Newfoundland dog

Quebec

Potatoes

Fruit

Canadian mounted police

Grain, timber, and mining
On the central plains of Canada, fields of wheat stretch as far as the eye can see. Timber and mining are important industries too. Grain, timber, and minerals are exported to other countries.

Quebec
The Canadian province of Quebec was once owned by France. It was taken over by the British in 1763, but three-quarters of the people still speak French as their main language. Many Quebécois would like to be independent from the rest of Canada.

The landforms and climate of the U.S. are very varied. To the west are the snowy peaks of the Rocky Mountains. On the plains of the midwest, summers are warm but winters are cold and snowy. In the southwest, there are hot, dry deserts. The islands of Hawaii are also part of the U.S.

THE UNITED STATES
◆ Washington, D.C. is the capital of the U.S. Find it and these large cities on the map.

United States of America

ATLANTIC OCEAN

PACIFIC OCEAN

1 Washington, D.C.   7 Chicago
2 New York   8 St. Louis
3 Boston   9 Dallas
4 Miami   10 Los Angeles
5 New Orleans   11 San Francisco
6 Detroit   12 Seattle

Rodeos
Rodeos are popular events in the West. Cowboys show off their skills at calf-roping, bull-riding, and riding untrained horses – the famous bucking broncos!

The United States

The United States of America is the richest and most powerful country in the world. It is made up of 50 states. Each state has its own local government and makes its own laws. English is the main language. Most people live in towns or cities, and work in shops, offices, factories, and service industries. The U.S. has some very big cities, such as New York and San Francisco, but there are large areas of the country where very few people live.

Surfing

Tourism

THE ISLANDS OF HAWAII

Volcanoes

Apples
Rocky Mountain goat
Airplane
Gray whale
Bison
Branding iron
Quail
Percupine
Wapiti
Devils Tower
Condor
Hare
Chipmunks
Giant redwood
Potatoes
Bighorn sheep
Grizzly bears
San Francisco
Salt Lake
Mustang
Speedway
Otters
Computer
Lynx
Las Vegas
Garibaldi fish
Fruit
Casino
Winter sports
Plums
Grand Canyon
Navajo weaving
Puma
Hollywood
Movies
Roadrunner
Elf owl
Pueblo houses
Elephant seals
Copper
Joshua tree
Cactus
Chuckwalla
Colorado River
Rattlesnake
Rio Grande River
Horned lizard
Yucca

To the moon!
In 1969 Apollo 11 blasted off from Cape Canaveral, taking men to the moon for the first time. Space and aircraft technology, computers, and military equipment are all important industries in the U.S.

The American Dream
During the last 500 years, more than 60 million people from all over the world have come to live in the United States. There are now 265 million people living in the United States.

The Pilgrim Fathers
The Pilgrim Fathers were among the first settlers from Europe. They set sail from England in the *Mayflower* in 1620. They hoped that in America they would be free to worship God in the way they wanted. They set up the colony of Plymouth, Massachusetts.

Wheat
Bald eagle
Halloween Pumpkin
Cranberries
Missouri River
Loon
Mount Rushmore
Beetroot
American black bear
Virginia deer
Dairy cow
Lake Superior
Trout
Salmon
Maple tree and syrup
Fir trees
Oak tree
Lake Huron
Niagara Falls
Lake Michigan
Cherries
Beaver
Acorns
Statue of Liberty
Barley
Farm
Gold
Car manufacture
Lake Erie
Farm
Tomatoes
Baseball
New York
Prairie dogs
Sunflowers
Basketball
Chicago
Pigs
Washington, D.C.
Skunks
St. Louis
Bourbon
Coal
Scissorbill
Corn
Opossum
Farm stead
Cereals
Raccoon
Horses
Turkey
American football
Coyote
Pike
Soya
Blueberries
Peanuts
Tobacco
Gas
Oil
Paddle boat
Cotton
Whale
Alligator turtle
Pelican
Oil
Rodeo
Lighthouse
Cotton
Heron
Oil
Cape Canaveral
Cattle
House
Snake
Snakebird
Tourism
Watermelon
Everglades
Cowboy
Mississippi River
New Orleans Jazz
Alligator
Marlin
Manatees
Spoonbill
Crane

Sports
Basketball and baseball developed in the U.S. They are now enjoyed by people in many countries. American football is not played much outside the U.S. Every year millions of Americans watch the championship finals, the Superbowl, on television.

◆ **LOOK AT THE BIG MAP.**

Can you find…
• the Statue of Liberty?
• five different kinds of wild animals?
• two large rivers and Niagara Falls?
• five different kinds of fruit?

17

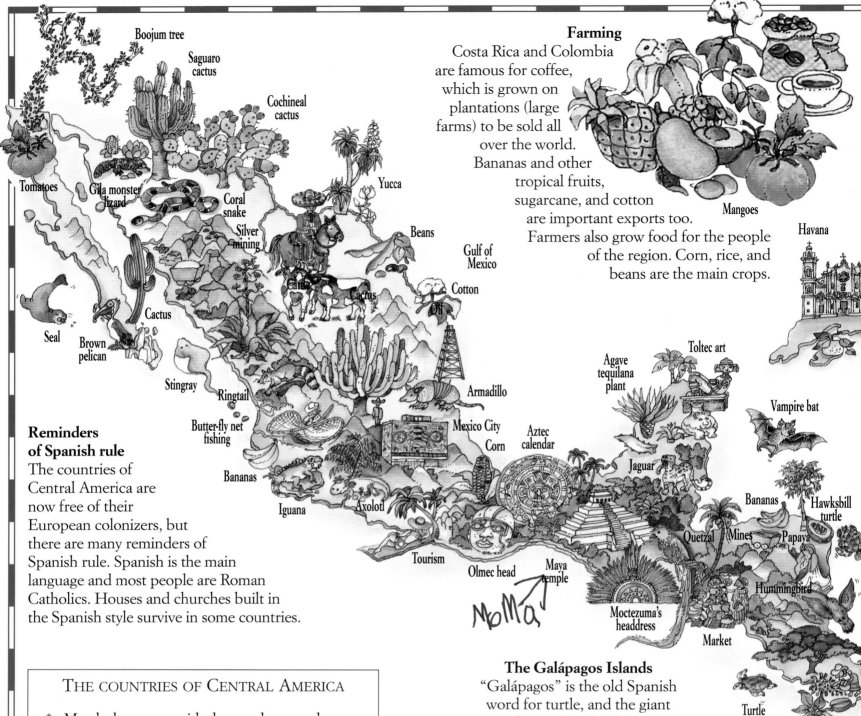

Farming

Costa Rica and Colombia are famous for coffee, which is grown on plantations (large farms) to be sold all over the world. Bananas and other tropical fruits, sugarcane, and cotton are important exports too.

Farmers also grow food for the people of the region. Corn, rice, and beans are the main crops.

Labels on map (top/left section):
Boojum tree · Saguaro cactus · Cochineal cactus · Yucca · Tomatoes · Gila monster lizard · Coral snake · Silver mining · Beans · Gulf of Mexico · Cactus · Cattle · Cactus · Cotton · Oil · Seal · Brown pelican · Stingray · Ringtail · Butterfly net fishing · Armadillo · Mexico City · Bananas · Iguana · Axolotl · Corn · Aztec calendar · Agave tequilana plant · Toltec art · Vampire bat · Jaguar · Bananas · Hawksbill turtle · Quetzal · Mines · Papaya · Tourism · Olmec head · Maya temple · Moctezuma's headdress · Hummingbird · Market · Turtle · Coffee · Havana

Reminders of Spanish rule

The countries of Central America are now free of their European colonizers, but there are many reminders of Spanish rule. Spanish is the main language and most people are Roman Catholics. Houses and churches built in the Spanish style survive in some countries.

The Galápagos Islands

"Galápagos" is the old Spanish word for turtle, and the giant turtles are the islands' most famous inhabitants.

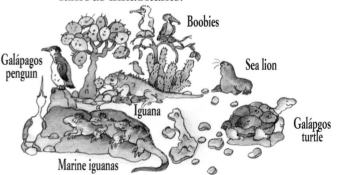

Labels: Boobies · Galápagos penguin · Sea lion · Iguana · Marine iguanas · Galápgos turtle

THE COUNTRIES OF CENTRAL AMERICA

◆ Match the names with the numbers on the map to find the capital cities of the larger countries.

Map labels: Mexico · Bahamas · Dominican Republic · Haiti · Puerto Rico · Cuba · Belize · Jamaica · Antigua & Barbuda · St. Christopher Nevis · Dominica · St. Lucia · Barbados · Guatemala · Honduras · Grenada · St. Vincent & the Grenadines · El Salvador · Nicaragua · Venezuela · Trinidad & Tobago · Costa Rica · Colombia · Guyana · French Guiana · Panama · Ecuador · Surinam

1 Mexico City	8 Panama City	14 Port of Spain
2 Belmopan	9 Havana	15 Quito
3 Guatemala City	10 Kingston	16 Bogotà
4 Tegucigalpa	11 Port-au-Prince	17 Caracas
5 San Salvador	12 Santo	18 Georgetown
6 Managua	Domingo	19 Paramaribo
7 San José	13 San Juan	20 Cayenne

Maya and Aztecs

The Maya lived in what are now Guatemala, Honduras, and Belize. They built cities with huge stone pyramids and temples. Later, the Aztecs controlled a large empire from the great city of Tenochtitlan. Their empire was destroyed by the Spanish in 1521.

◆ LOOK AT THE BIG MAP.

Can you find...

• three examples of Maya or Aztec art?
• ten different wild animals?
• four different types of fruit?
• the Galápagos Islands?
• the Panama Canal?

Most of Central America is hilly or mountainous, although there are humid swamps along the eastern coasts. There are tropical rain forests in Central America and northern South America. The region lies on a fault in the earth's crust, so there are many volcanoes here and earthquakes can cause terrible destruction.

Mexico, Central America, and Northern South America

The countries of Central America form a "bridge" linking North and South America. Most people in the region have Native American and European ancestors, because much of the area was ruled by Spain in colonial times. Many people work as farmers, or in workshops producing clothing, shoes, and furniture. In Mexico there are more people who work in factories.

Brown pelican

Tropical fruit

Tourism

Cuban solenodon

Cuban cigar

Sugarcane

Rum

Sailfish

Shark

Diego

Coral reefs

Sugarcane

Caracas

Scarlet ibis

Piranha fish

Banana

Salt mines

Oil

Coconuts

Capybara

Mangroves

Harpy eagle

Panama canal

Emerald

Cattle farming

Orinoco River

Hoatzin

Bird spider

Cocoa

Hawler monkey

King vulture

Cayman

Butterfly

Prawns

Gold

Orchid

Angel Falls

Ocelot

Spectacled bear

Pre-Colombian statue

Bogotá

Toucans

Frogs

Sloth

Coati

mask

Coffee

Jaguar

Scarlet macaw

Wooly monkey

Boa constrictor

Two-toed anteater

Volcanoes

Poison-arrow frog

Tapir

Panama hat

Jungle animals

Monkeys, toucans, and parakeets chatter in the trees of the Colombian jungle. Boa constrictors slither along the branches. Jaguars, the American big cats, stalk their prey. Capybaras – the world's largest rodents – and anteaters shuffle around the jungle floor. Flesh-eating piranhas and crocodiles lurk in the rivers.

South America and Antarctica

Almost half the population of South America lives in Brazil. The main language is Portuguese, because Brazil was once ruled by Portugal. Other countries were ruled by Spain, so Spanish is the main language in the rest of the region. In big cities, such as Rio de Janeiro and Buenos Aires, many people work in factories. Outside the cities farming is the main occupation. Beyond the southern tip of South America lies the frozen continent of Antarctica.

The Andes Mountains run down the western side of South America. To the east, the great Amazon River flows through lush tropical rain forests. In Argentina there are large areas of open grassland, called the pampas, which are good for farming and raising cattle. The northern part of the continent is warm and wet, but it is cold high in the Andes and in southern Argentina and Chile.

Antarctica

Antarctica is a huge, frozen continent. Very few creatures can survive the extreme cold. Seals and penguins live around the coasts and the oceans are rich in fish. The enormous blue whale, the largest mammal in the world, lives in these icy waters. No one lives permanently in Antarctica, although some scientists stay for a few months to carry out research.

◆ LOOK AT THE BIG MAPS.
Can you find…
• the Amazon River?
• six colorful birds?
• four different whales?
• the city of Rio de Janeiro?
• the South Pole?
• four different seals that live in Antarctica?

Cotton

Llamas
Together with alpaca, vicuña, and guanaco, llamas are members of the camel family. They are important to the people of the Andes. They carry loads, provide meat for food, and wool to make clothes, rugs, and ropes.

Rain forests
The Amazon rain forest covers 40 per-cent of Brazil's total area. Millions of plant and animal species live in the forest. Although the rain forest is important for world climate, large areas are cut down each year to clear land for farming and to provide timber.

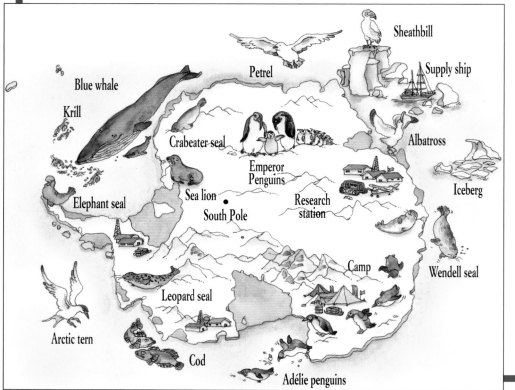

Sheathbill
Supply ship
Petrel
Blue whale
Krill
Crabeater seal
Albatross
Emperor Penguins
Sea lion
South Pole
Research station
Iceberg
Elephant seal
Camp
Wendell seal
Leopard seal
Arctic tern
Cod
Adélie penguins

THE COUNTRIES OF SOUTH AMERICA

◆ Find the capital cities of each country.

Colombia, Ecuador, Venezuela, Guyana, French Guiana, and Suriname are also part of South America. They are on pp. 18–19.

1 Brasilia
2 Asunción
3 Lima
4 Santiago
5 Buenos Aires
6 La Paz
7 Montevideo

ATLANTIC OCEAN
Peru
Brazil
Bolivia
Paraguay
Chile
Uruguay
Argentina
ANTARCTIC OCEAN

Monkeys

Rubber production

Spatuletail

Condor

Oil

Vultures

Amazon River

Frigate bird

Cotton

Sailing

Brazil nuts

Amazon River dolphin

Tourism

Water lily

Matamata

Cashew nuts

Turtles

Toucans

Gold

Moche art

Bullfrog

Coffee

Golden lion tamarin

Giant armadillo

Peccaries

Tobacco

Cock-of-the-rock

Pirarucu fish

Sugarcane

Machu Pichu

Butterfly

Emerald boa

Hyacinth macaw

Church of our Lady of Carmo

Bananas

Cormorants

Soccer

Tapir

Brasilia

Cacao

Lima Cathedral

Reed boat

Cayman

Brazilian giant otter

Coffee

Salt mines

Llama

Puya

Jaguar

Anaconda

Mines

Vicuña

Horned toad

Citrus fruit

Tropic bird

Industry

Weaving

Pelican

Alpaca

Carnival

Guanaco

Pampas deer

Industry

Rio de Janeiro

Timber

Fishing boat

Rhea

Iguaçu Falls

Lapis lazuli

Vampire bats

Giant anteater

Grapes

Puma

Sheep farming

Southern right-whale

Cattle

Gaucho

Cereals

Monkey puzzle tree

Cereals

Chinchilla

Farm

Notro tree

Armadillo

Seal

Flamingoes

Sea lion

Killer whale

Patagonian hare

Squid

Magellanic penguin

Albatross

Falkland Islands

Sperm whale

Crab

Lenga tree

Rockhopper penguins

Cape Horn

Carnival!

Every year a great carnival takes place in Rio de Janeiro in Brazil. People dress up in spectacular costumes and parade through the streets on decorated floats. Music and dancing go on for five days.

Gauchos

Gauchos are South American cowboys. They herd cattle on the pampas in Argentina.

Northern Europe

Northern Europe is composed of the four Nordic countries of Finland, Norway, Sweden, and Denmark, as well as the United Kingdom, Ireland, and Iceland. There is a lot of industry, and most people work in factories, offices, shops, and service industries. Fishing and farming are also important activities. English is the main language in the United Kingdom and Ireland. The Nordic countries each have their own language.

Tourism
Tourism is important in Scotland. People come to see the beautiful scenery and to enjoy Scottish traditions, such as bagpipe music and tartan kilts.

A great past
There are many old castles, churches, and stately homes in the United Kingdom and Ireland.

The countries of **Northern Europe** have cool climates with high rainfall. They have long, cold winters, particularly in the north. In Iceland and the north of the Nordic countries it stays dark all day during the winter months. In summer, it is light even at night.

ARCTIC OCEAN
ATLANTIC OCEAN
Europe
Africa

Puffin
Volcano
Waterfall
Walrus
Seals
Killer whale

Faroe Islands

Sheep
Shetland Islands

Tweed
Fisherman
Duck
Orkney Islands
Hebrides Islands
Cormorant
Whisky
Bagpipes
Kilts
Loch Ness monster

Sea gulls
Fisherman
Celtic cross
Castle
Hake
Sheep
Lobster
Irish setter
Horse
Collie
Shipbuilding yards
Ceramics
Heather
Isle of Man
Factory
Cottage
Guinness
Soccer
Beer
Peat
Potatoes
Barley
Mines
Woods
Cow
Horse riding
Student
Fox
Herrings
Welsh costume
Manor house
Daffodils
Stonehenge
Tower Bridge
Thames River
Salisbury Cathedral
Badger
Fish
Catfish
Channel Islands

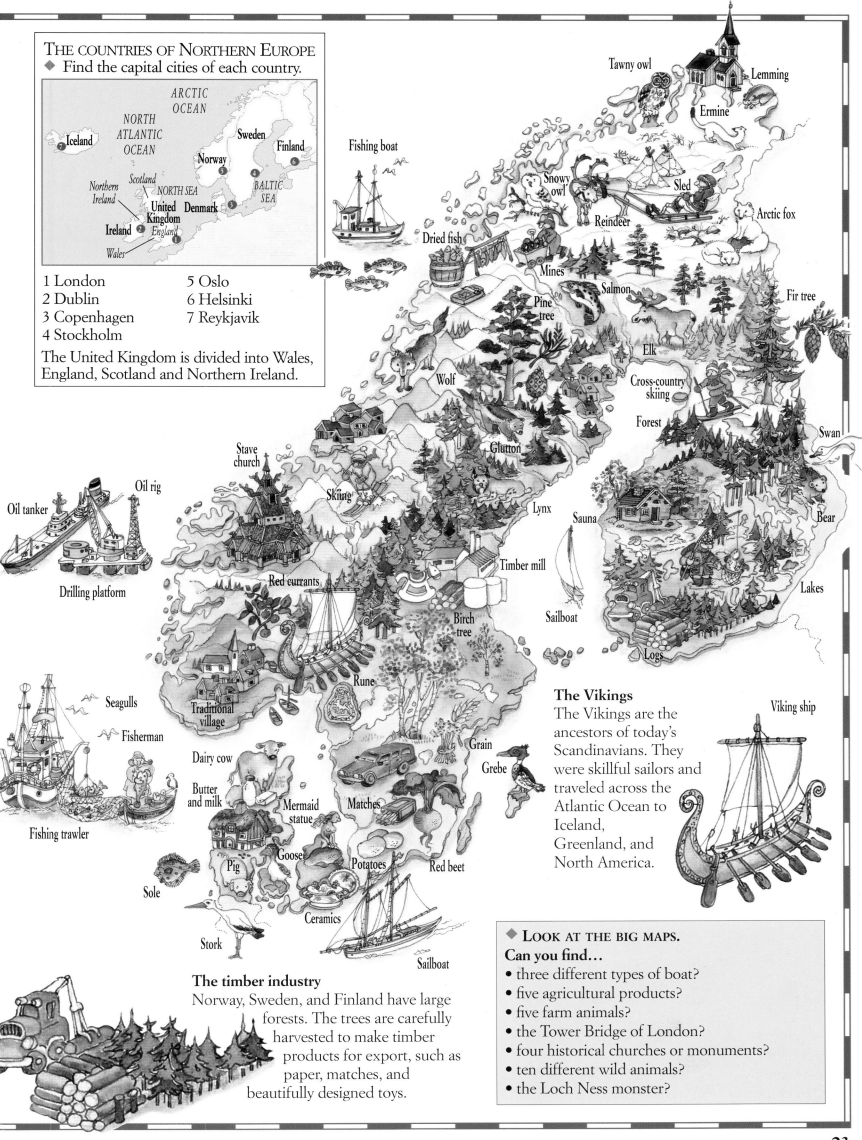

ARCTIC OCEAN

NORTH ATLANTIC OCEAN

Iceland ⑦

NORTH ATLANTIC OCEAN

Sweden

Norway

Finland

Scotland

Northern Ireland

NORTH SEA

BALTIC SEA

United Kingdom

Denmark

Ireland ②

England ①

Wales

1 London
2 Dublin
3 Copenhagen
4 Stockholm
5 Oslo
6 Helsinki
7 Reykjavik

The United Kingdom is divided into Wales, England, Scotland and Northern Ireland.

Tawny owl

Lemming

Ermine

Snowy owl

Sled

Reindeer

Arctic fox

Fishing boat

Dried fish

Mines

Salmon

Pine tree

Fir tree

Elk

Cross-country skiing

Wolf

Forest

Swan

Stave church

Glutton

Skiing

Lynx

Sauna

Bear

Oil rig

Oil tanker

Drilling platform

Timber mill

Sailboat

Lakes

Red currants

Logs

Birch tree

Rune

The Vikings

The Vikings are the ancestors of today's Scandinavians. They were skillful sailors and traveled across the Atlantic Ocean to Iceland, Greenland, and North America.

Viking ship

Seagulls

Fisherman

Traditional village

Dairy cow

Grain

Grebe

Butter and milk

Matches

Mermaid statue

Goose

Potatoes

Red beet

Fishing trawler

Sole

Pig

Ceramics

Stork

Sailboat

The timber industry

Norway, Sweden, and Finland have large forests. The trees are carefully harvested to make timber products for export, such as paper, matches, and beautifully designed toys.

◆ **LOOK AT THE BIG MAPS.**
Can you find…
• three different types of boat?
• five agricultural products?
• five farm animals?
• the Tower Bridge of London?
• four historical churches or monuments?
• ten different wild animals?
• the Loch Ness monster?

Central Europe

Most people in Central Europe live in towns and cities and work in offices and factories. The factories produce a wide range of goods, from cars in Germany to watches and medical instruments in Switzerland. Farming is also important in some areas, especially southern Germany and parts of the Netherlands. German is spoken in several countries but each country has its own language.

◆ **LOOK AT THE BIG MAP.**
Can you find…
• Vienna and the Lippizaner horse?
• two large ports?
• five wild animals?
• three different types of food?

Beer and wine
Barley and hops are grown in Germany to make beer. A famous beer festival, the *Oktoberfest*, is held each year in Munich to celebrate the harvest. There are also many vineyards where grapes are grown to make into wine.

THE COUNTRIES OF CENTRAL EUROPE
◆ Find the capital cities of each country.

1 Amsterdam
2 Brussels
3 Luxembourg
4 Berlin
5 Bern
6 Vienna
7 Vaduz
8 Warsaw
9 Prague
10 Bratislava
11 Budapest

The Rhine

The Rhine is the biggest river in Western Europe. It flows for 865 miles from the Swiss Alps to the Netherlands, where it reaches the North Sea. Barges loaded with cargo travel along the Rhine, calling at inland ports, such as Cologne. In Switzerland, the energy of its rushing waters is used to produce hydroelectric power.

Vienna

Vienna is the capital of Austria. It was once the center of a powerful empire. Beautiful old buildings, such as the Imperial Palace, are reminders of its past. Acrobatic Lippizaner horses are trained at the Spanish Riding School. The Vienna State Opera is one of the most famous opera houses in the world.

East and West

Poland, the Czech Republic, Slovakia, Hungary, and eastern Germany were ruled by Communist governments under the influence of the Soviet Union until the late 1980s. Germany was divided into two separate countries. When the Communist government of East Germany collapsed in 1989, Germany became one country again. People flocked to the wall that divided Berlin and tore it down.

The landscape of Central Europe is varied. The Netherlands is very flat – parts of the country are below sea level and have to be drained by a system of dikes. Switzerland and Austria, in the south, are mountainous. The mountains here are the Alps. The Carpathian Mountains are further east, in southern Poland and Slovakia. The Rhine River and the Danube River flow across the center of the region.

Map labels: Stork, Container loader, Port of Gdansk, Black stork, Cod, Herring, Gdansk, Elk, Amber, Vistula River, Farming, European bison, Oder River, Potatoes, Beet, Lapwings, Brandenburg gate, Coal mining, Red deer, Roe deer, Grey heron, Cuckoo, Carp, Elm tree, Barley, Crows, Wheat, Dormouse, Owl, Icon, Warsaw, Wooden house, Hare, Industry, Kraków, Mole, Dresden, Mountaineering, Chamois goat, Wooden church, Traditional costume, Otter, Lynx, Prague, Bohemian crystal, Thermal springs, Timber, Brown bear, Coal, Industry, Wild boars, Barley, Grapes, Bratislava, Industry, Lippizaner horse, Vienna, Wine, Shepherd, Spoonbill, Catfish, Budapest, Hungarian horseman, Vulture, Red beeet, Danube River, Corn, Paprika, Polecat, Water vole

↓ switserLanb

Mediterranean Europe

Many parts of Mediterranean Europe have big cities, and a lot of industry. The people in these areas work in factories, offices, and shops. They have modern lifestyles. In some other areas the people live as farmers. They lead traditional lives, just as their parents and grandparents did.

Punch
The famous puppet called Punch first came from Italy. In Italian he is called *Pulcinella*.

The countries of **Mediterranean Europe** face across the Mediterranean Sea towards Africa. The region has many mountains. The largest ranges are the Alps in northern Italy, and the Pyrenees between Spain and France. There are many rivers, the largest of which is the Loire River, in France. The winters are quite mild and wet, while the summers are hot and dry. Some large forests are found in the north. There are many islands in the Mediterranean Sea. The Italian islands of Sicily and Sardinia are the largest.

Europe
ATLANTIC OCEAN
Asia
Africa
INDIAN OCEAN

Mont Saint-Michel
Port
Oysters
Seine River
Car factory
Goose
Hedgehog
Farm
Mines
Notre Dame
Cow
Champagne
Loire River
Snail
Chateau
Cheese
Acorn
TGV
Garonne River
Ceramics
Tunnel
Wine
Mont Blanc
Surfer
Cave paintings
Fox
Apples
Owl
Eagle
Lavender
Santiago de Compostela
Camargue horse
Vineyards
Pyrenees
Rhone River
Partridges
Hare
Deer
Sardines
Douro River
Bull fighter
Sagrada Familia Church
Duck
Tagus River
Escorial Palace
Oak
Wind mills
Ebro River
Lobster
Tourist
Sheep
Balearic Islands
Seal
Lynx
Heron
Apricots
Guadiana River
Guadalquivir River
Alhambra
Tuna
Flamenco dancer

◆ **LOOK AT THE BIG MAP.**
Can you see...
- five different wild animals?
- two tall mountain ranges?
- five different kinds of food?
- the Leaning Tower of Pisa?

26

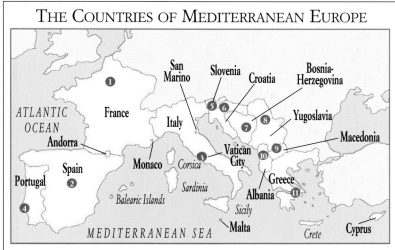

THE COUNTRIES OF MEDITERRANEAN EUROPE

ATLANTIC OCEAN

France
Andorra
Spain
Portugal

San Marino
Slovenia
Croatia
Bosnia-Herzegovina
Italy
Yugoslavia
Monaco
Corsica
Vatican City
Macedonia
Sardinia
Greece
Balearic Islands
Albania
Sicily
Malta
Crete
Cyprus

MEDITERRANEAN SEA

◆ Match the names with the numbers on the map to find the capital cities of each country.

1 Paris	**4** Lisbon	**7** Sarajevo	**10** Tirana
2 Madrid	**5** Ljubljana	**8** Belgrade	**11** Athens
3 Rome	**6** Zagreb	**9** Skopje	

Transportation

There are many busy highways and railroads. Airports link all the major cities. In France there are trains called T.G.V. that go faster than any other trains in the world.

Ancient civilizations

The first great civilizations of Europe, including Ancient Greece and Rome, grew up around the Mediterranean Sea.

Traditions

There are strong traditions in Mediterranean Europe. On special days people dress up, prepare feasts, and listen to music or dance. They celebrate being together as part of a group. Flamenco dancing is a tradition in Spain.

Agriculture

The main crops grown are grapes, olives, vegetables, grain, fruit, and timber. Fishing is also important in most countries.

Ibex
The Alps
Venice
Chestnut
Mushrooms
Factory
Violin
Badger
o River
Gondola
Eel
Cypresses
Bear
Wild boar
Hoopoe
Leaning Tower of Pisa
Squirrel
Porcupine
Orthodox Church
Figs
Trulli houses
Pasta
Corsica
St. Peter's Cathedral
Bee
Greek Orthodox priest
Tiber River
Sheep
Pizza
Goat
Punch
Tomatoes
Bat
Sardinia
Fishing boat
Mount Etna
Wolf
Ancient Greek temple
Indian fig
Squid
Olives
Swordfish
Ancient mask
Citrus fruit
Snake goddess
Sicily
Dolphins
Turtle
Ancient vase
Crete

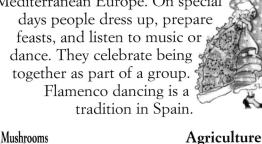

Eastern Europe

Russia is the biggest country in Eastern Europe – in fact, only part of Russia is in Europe and the rest stretches east across Siberia towards the Pacific Ocean. In the west, along the Baltic Sea, are the small states of Latvia, Lithuania, and Estonia. Many people in this region work in factories in towns and cities. Farming is important in southern Russia, on the steppes (plains). Russian is the main language, although the people of the Baltic States have their own languages.

◆ **LOOK AT THE BIG MAP.**
Can you find...
- a traditional musical instrument called the balalaika?
- five agricultural products?
- five farm animals?
- three different churches?
- ten different wild animals?

Moscow

Moscow is the capital of Russia. The famous Kremlin is a collection of palaces and cathedrals that were built in the fifteenth century. It is the traditional center of the Russian government. Outside the Kremlin is Red Square. The body of Lenin, the first Communist ruler, is preserved in a mausoleum here.

Wildlife

Elks, bears, wolves, and smaller animals, such as sable and martens, live in the great northern forests. Foxes, bustards, and eagles live on the steppes. Small mammals such as marmots live in burrows, to escape the keen eyes of predators on the open plains.

Russian ballet

Russian ballet dancers are among the best in the world. Dancers of the Bolshoi and Kirov companies perform ballets such as *Swan Lake* and *Sleeping Beauty*. The music for many ballets was written by Tchaikovsky, a Russian composer.

Industries

Russia has many of the raw materials needed for heavy industry and manufacturing: coal, gas, and oil for power, and iron ore for making steel. Russian factories produce heavy machinery, such as farm equipment, railroad engines, and cars. Mining for minerals such as cobalt, lead, and zinc is also important.

The Cossacks

The Cossacks lived in southern Russia, around the Don and Volga rivers. They were famous for their skill as soldiers and horsemen. They were also famous for their energetic dances. They would squat down with arms folded and fling out their legs. Sometimes they danced with swords.

THE COUNTRIES OF EASTERN EUROPE

◆ Match the names with the numbers on the map to find the capital cities of each country.

1 Moscow	7 Chisinau
2 Tallinn	8 Bucharest
3 Riga	9 Sofia
4 Vilnius	10 Tbilisi
5 Minsk	11 Yerevan
6 Kiev	12 Baku

Caviar
Caviar – the salty eggs, or "roe," of fish called sturgeon – is a great delicacy. It is a very expensive food. The finest caviar comes from the sturgeon of the Caspian Sea.

The summers in Eastern Europe are mild but winters are cold and snowy. The far north of Russia is bitterly cold. The Ural Mountains mark the boundary between Europe and Asia. Half of Russia is covered in forests of conifers – the taiga. Major rivers such as the Don and the Volga flow south to the Black Sea. The steppes in the south of the region are good for growing wheat and other cereal crops.

Religion
The Russian Orthodox Church is a branch of Christianity. It has been the main religion in Russia for over 1,000 years. Many Russian Christians have icons – small paintings of saints or of Mary and the baby Jesus – in their homes, which they use as a focus for their prayers.

Tern
Ship
Big Bluebill
Harp seal
Reindeer
Ptarmigan
Northern hawk owl
Scorpion fish
Arctic hare
Reindeer
Lemmings
Dwarf birch
Arctic fox
Redshank
Mink
Elk
Ural Mountains
Northern Dvina River
Balalaika
Salmon
Chessboard
Deer
Eagle
Sheldducks
Matrioshka dolls
Wood grouse
Brown bears
St. Petersburg
Stave church
Weasel
Mines
Ferry
Russian wolfhound
Tallinn
ic Sea
of Riga
Timber
Silver birch trees
Dacha
Icon
Industry
Marten
Flax
Red beet
Long-eared bat
Pike
Oil
Gold
Potatoes
St. Basil's cathedral
Samovar
Factory
Coal
Pigs
Russian ballet
Russian Orthodox priest
Wheat
Vodka
Coal
Beaver
Shrew
Cow
Geese
Wheat
Farmhouse
Hamster
Sunflower
Corn
Cossacks
Castor oil plant
Viper
Monastery
Port of Odessa
Kiev
Volga River
Bucharest
Don River
Volgograd
Rose
Pelican
Porpoise
Coal
Industry
Shepherd
Gas
Sturgeon
Tourism
Castle
Cruise boat
Fishing
Farming
Tobacco
Tea
Fruit
Sheep
Perch
Rugs
Oil rigs
Cotton

29

Northern Africa

Most of northern Africa is covered by the Sahara Desert. The majority of people live near the coasts where it is not too hot and dry. To the north, most people speak the Arabic language, although French and English are common too. Islam is the main religion. Many people live in the country and work as farmers, although there are also some very large cities. Cairo, the capital city of Egypt, is the largest city in Africa.

The Sahara Desert
The Sahara Desert is the largest desert in the world. It covers more than a quarter of the African continent. It is growing larger every year.

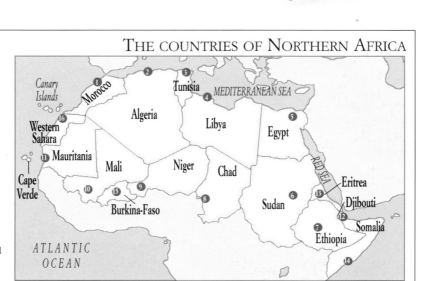

Tuna fish
Cedar tree
Minaret
Citrus fruit
Figs
Tile
Shepherd
Dates
Carpet
Tourism
Teapot
Date palm
Goats and sheep
Oil well
Mines
Tuareg tent
Desert palms
Gum arabic
Dogfish
Tuareg
Rock paintings
Snake
Antelope
Jeep
Saddle
Mosque
Fisherman
Rice
Baskets
Djenne mosque
Millet
Sorghum
Village
Cotton
Peanuts
Niger River
Market

The Islamic religion
The majority of people in northern Africa are Muslims. They believe in Allah and follow the Islamic religion. There are loud calls to prayer five times each day. Believers kneel on prayer mats, facing Mecca in the east, and bend down to touch their heads on the ground as they pray. There are many beautiful mosques.

◆ Match the names with the numbers on the map to find the capital cities of each country.

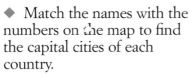

1 Rabat	9 Niamey
2 Algiers	10 Bamako
3 Tunis	11 Nouakchott
4 Tripoli	12 Djibouti
5 Cairo	13 Asmara
6 Khartoum	14 Mogadishu
7 Addis Ababa	15 Ouagadougou
8 N'Djamena	16 Al-Aioun

THE COUNTRIES OF NORTHERN AFRICA

Canary Islands
Morocco
Tunisia
MEDITERRANEAN SEA
Western Sahara
Algeria
Libya
Egypt
Mauritania
Cape Verde
Mali
Niger
Chad
RED SEA
Eritrea
Burkina-Faso
Sudan
Djibouti
Somalia
Ethiopia
ATLANTIC OCEAN

The first people
Africa is sometimes called the "cradle of humanity" because traces of the first human beings have been found there. Many objects, like the stone cutter above, date to millions of years ago.

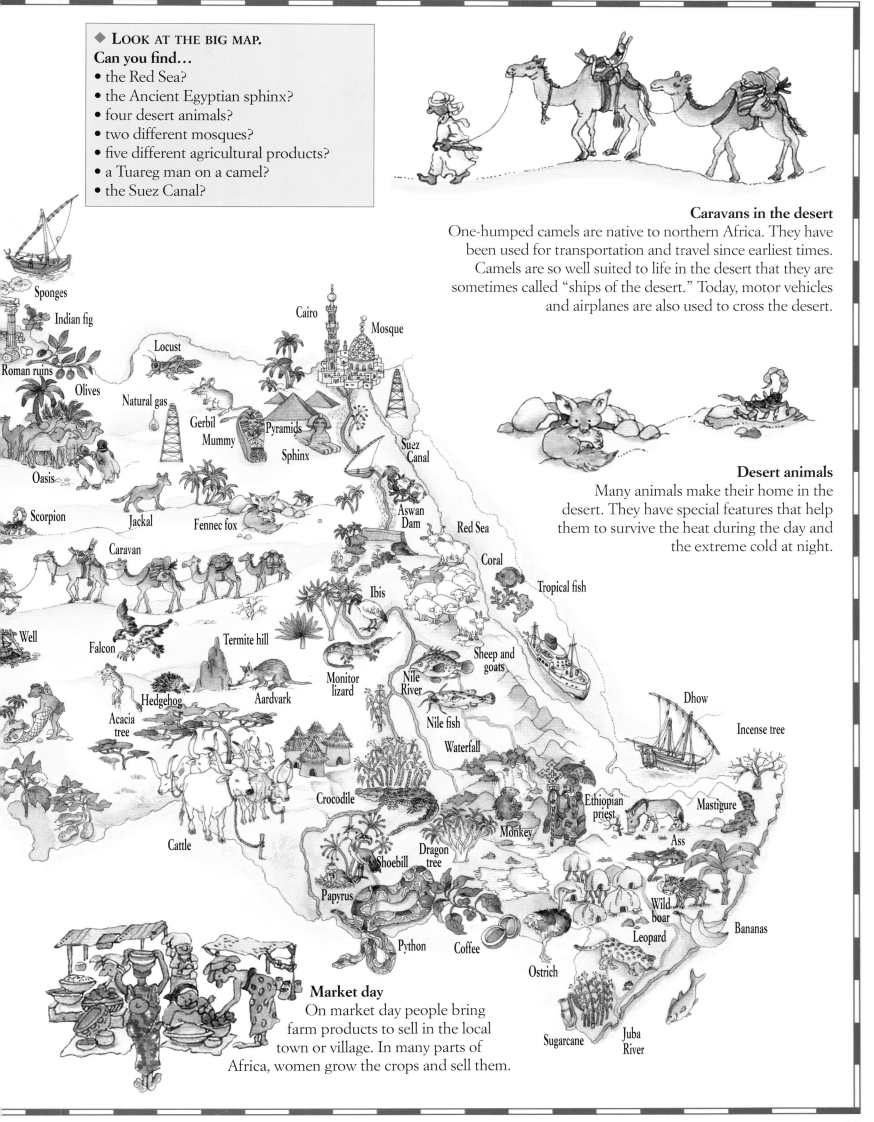

◆ **LOOK AT THE BIG MAP.**
Can you find…
- the Red Sea?
- the Ancient Egyptian sphinx?
- four desert animals?
- two different mosques?
- five different agricultural products?
- a Tuareg man on a camel?
- the Suez Canal?

Caravans in the desert
One-humped camels are native to northern Africa. They have been used for transportation and travel since earliest times. Camels are so well suited to life in the desert that they are sometimes called "ships of the desert." Today, motor vehicles and airplanes are also used to cross the desert.

Desert animals
Many animals make their home in the desert. They have special features that help them to survive the heat during the day and the extreme cold at night.

Sponges

Indian fig

Locust

Cairo

Mosque

Roman ruins

Olives

Natural gas

Gerbil

Mummy

Pyramids

Sphinx

Suez Canal

Oasis

Scorpion

Jackal

Fennec fox

Aswan Dam

Red Sea

Coral

Tropical fish

Caravan

Ibis

Well

Falcon

Termite hill

Monitor lizard

Nile River

Sheep and goats

Dhow

Incense tree

Hedgehog

Aardvark

Nile fish

Acacia tree

Waterfall

Crocodile

Ethiopian priest

Mastigure

Cattle

Monkey

Ass

Shoebill

Dragon tree

Papyrus

Wild boar

Bananas

Python

Coffee

Leopard

Ostrich

Market day
On market day people bring farm products to sell in the local town or village. In many parts of Africa, women grow the crops and sell them.

Sugarcane

Juba River

31

Southern Africa

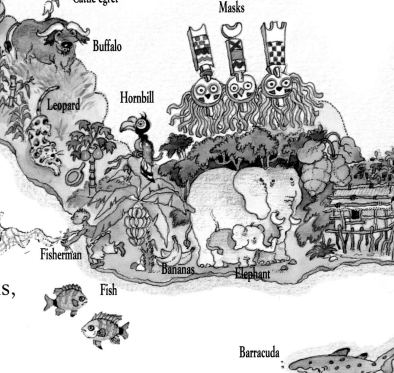

Most people in southern Africa live in rural areas. They earn their living as farmers by growing crops and raising cattle. Many others live in cities. They work in shops, offices, factories, and mines. They speak many different languages. Southern Africa has huge forests and savannas with many wild animals, including elephants, lions, giraffes, chimpanzees, and gorillas.

Wildlife reserves
Many wild animals live in reserves where they are safe from poachers. People from all over the world visit Africa to see the animals.

The first humans
Africa is the birthplace of humans. The first people lived in Kenya and Tanzania millions of years ago. From here they spread all over the world. Rock paintings left by early peoples tell us something about their life.

Primal religions
Many African people believe in a world of spirits and gods. They have special ceremonies, with dance and song to worship the gods. Sometimes they wear masks during these ceremonies.

Madagascar
The huge island of Madagascar lies off the coast of Southern Africa. It has been isolated from the continent for millions of years. It has unique plants and animals. The ring-tailed lemur, a distant relative of the monkey, lives only on Madagascar.

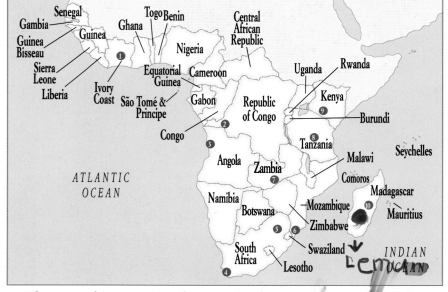

THE COUNTRIES OF SOUTHERN AFRICA

◆ There are thirty-three countries in Southern Africa. The Republic of Congo is the biggest. South Africa is the richest.

Madagascar is a large island that was once part of Africa. The red dots with numbers in them on the brown map show some of the largest cities in this part of the world. Find the number on the map to see where they are.

1 Yamoussoukro
2 Kinshasa
3 Luanda
4 Cape Town
5 Johannesburg
6 Maputo
7 Lusaka
8 Dodoma
9 Nairobi
10 Antananarivo

Southern Africa, also called Subsaharan Africa, lies below the Sahara Desert, and between the Indian and Atlantic oceans. There is tropical rain forest near the equator. Further south there are grasslands (called savanna) and deserts. The climate is hot or warm with enough rain, except in the Namib and Kalahari deserts, which are very dry. The largest rivers are the Congo, the Zambezi, and the Niger.

◆ **LOOK AT THE BIG MAP.**
Can you find…
• a traditional African village?
• ten different wild animals?
• two large rivers?
• three different masks?
• five different trees?
• Victoria Falls?
• Mount Kilimanjaro?

Mineral wealth
Many countries have rich deposits of minerals, such as copper, gold, tin, and diamonds.

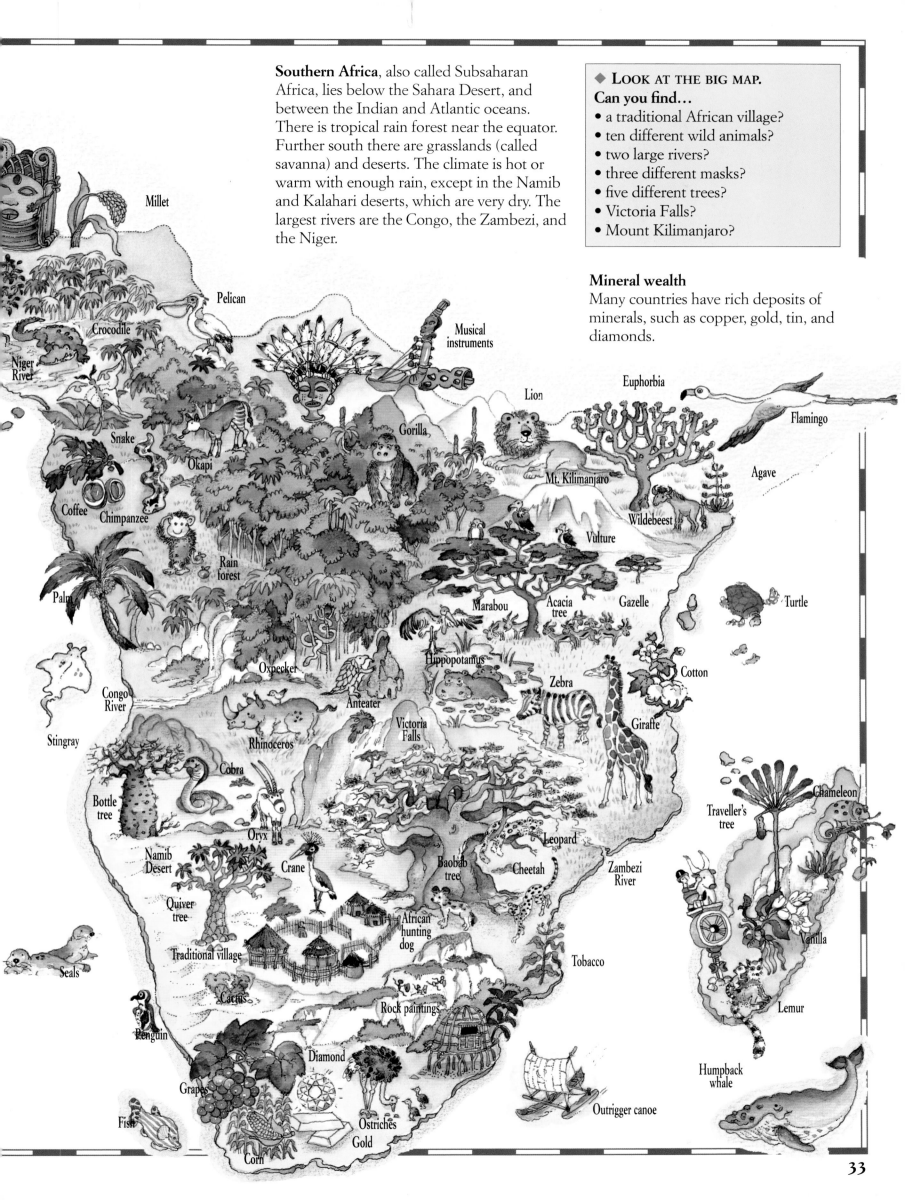

Millet

Pelican

Crocodile

Niger River

Musical instruments

Lion

Euphorbia

Flamingo

Snake

Gorilla

Okapi

Mt. Kilimanjaro

Agave

Coffee

Chimpanzee

Wildebeest

Vulture

Rain forest

Palm

Marabou

Acacia tree

Gazelle

Turtle

Oxpecker

Hippopotamus

Cotton

Congo River

Anteater

Zebra

Giraffe

Stingray

Rhinoceros

Victoria Falls

Cobra

Bottle tree

Oryx

Leopard

Chameleon

Namib Desert

Crane

Baobab tree

Cheetah

Zambezi River

Traveller's tree

Quiver tree

African hunting dog

Vanilla

Traditional village

Cactus

Tobacco

Lemur

Seals

Rock paintings

Penguin

Diamond

Grapes

Humpback whale

Fish

Outrigger canoe

Ostriches
Gold

Corn

33

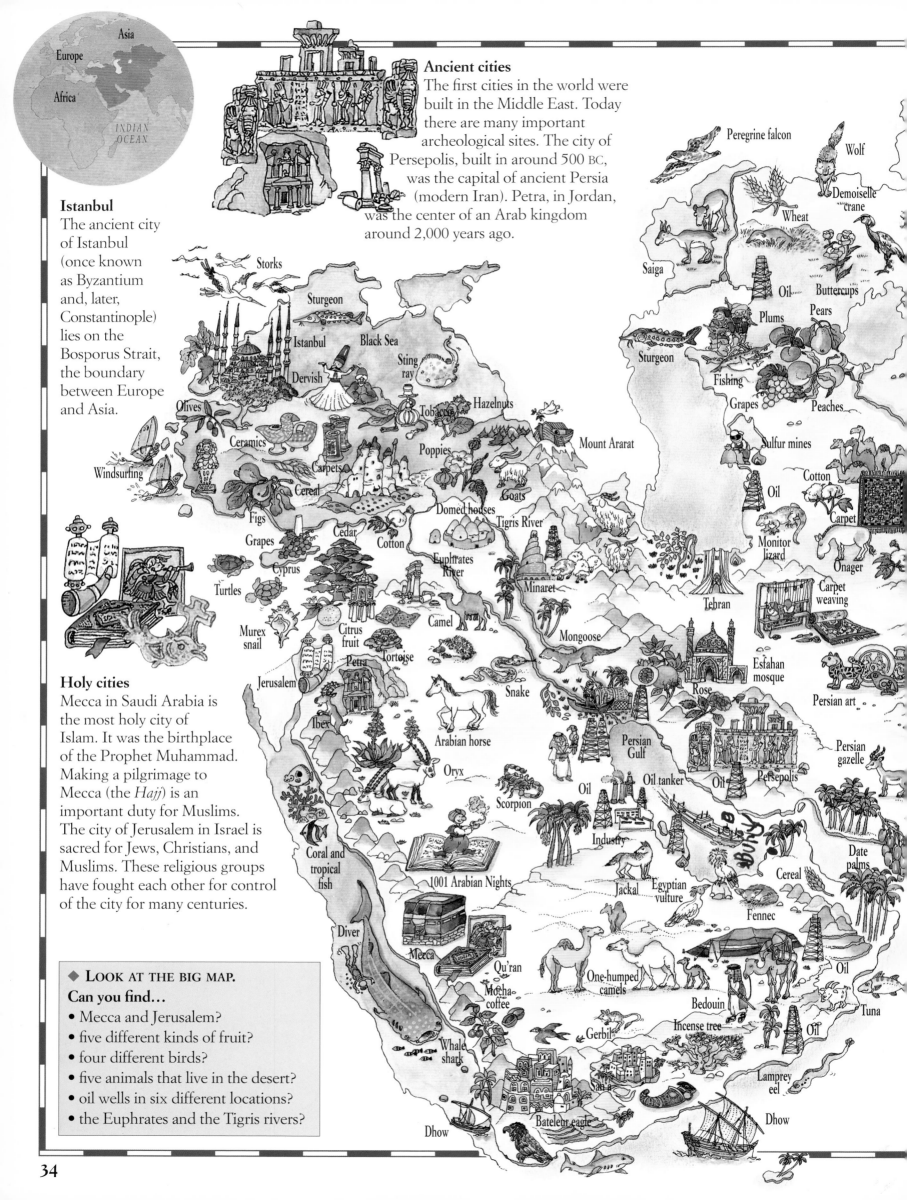

Ancient cities
The first cities in the world were built in the Middle East. Today there are many important archeological sites. The city of Persepolis, built in around 500 BC, was the capital of ancient Persia (modern Iran). Petra, in Jordan, was the center of an Arab kingdom around 2,000 years ago.

Istanbul
The ancient city of Istanbul (once known as Byzantium and, later, Constantinople) lies on the Bosporus Strait, the boundary between Europe and Asia.

Holy cities
Mecca in Saudi Arabia is the most holy city of Islam. It was the birthplace of the Prophet Muhammad. Making a pilgrimage to Mecca (the *Hajj*) is an important duty for Muslims. The city of Jerusalem in Israel is sacred for Jews, Christians, and Muslims. These religious groups have fought each other for control of the city for many centuries.

◆ LOOK AT THE BIG MAP.
Can you find...
• Mecca and Jerusalem?
• five different kinds of fruit?
• four different birds?
• five animals that live in the desert?
• oil wells in six different locations?
• the Euphrates and the Tigris rivers?

The Middle East and Central Asia

Much of the Middle East is very hot and dry, so most people live where they can find water. Many people work as farmers. Others work in the oil industry, especially in Saudi Arabia and the countries around the Persian Gulf. Most of the Middle Eastern peoples are Arabs. Their religion is Islam. The modern country of Israel was founded in 1948. It is a Jewish nation. The peoples of Central Asia are mainly Muslims. Most live as farmers, although industry is growing too.

Oil

Around the Persian Gulf oil collects naturally in underground pools. Eight million barrels of oil a day are produced in Saudi Arabia, the region's biggest producer. It is transported by pipeline or in huge oil tankers to countries around the world. Oil has brought great wealth to some of the Middle Eastern states.

Hot, dry, sandy deserts cover large areas of the Middle East. When rain does fall, it often comes in heavy downpours which cause sudden floods. Summers are very hot, but in the central regions winters can be very cold. Along the Mediterranean coasts and in the valleys of the Tigris and Euphrates rivers there is fertile land that is good for farming. The countries of Central Asia have many deserts and high, rugged mountains.

Growing cotton

Cotton production is an important industry in the central Asian states of Tajikistan, Turkmenistan, and Uzbekistan.

Bazaars

Markets in Middle Eastern towns are called bazaars. Twisting narrow streets are crowded with traders selling their wares. Bazaars are often covered by canopies or a roof, to protect people from the hot sun.

Map labels: Bobacs · Cereals · Cereals · Cereals · Sand grouse · Golden hamster · Sunflower · Mining · Gold · Mines · Space base · Kiangs · Lake Balkhash · Shepherd · Ground squirrel · Goats · Desert dormouse · Sheep · Yak · Samarkand · Industry · Nomads' tents · Bearded vulture · Afghan hound · Lapis lazuli · Melons · Antelope · Nomads' tents · Cotton · Pallas' cat · Carpet

The Countries of the Middle East and Central Asia

◆ Match the names with the numbers on the map to find the capital cities of each country.

1 Amman
2 Jerusalem
3 Damascus
4 Beirut
5 Ankara
6 Baghdad
7 Tehran
8 Ashgabat
9 Tashkent
10 Astana
11 Bishkek
12 Dushanbe
13 Kabul
14 Islamabad

15 Kuwait City	17 Doha	19 Muscat
16 Riyadh	18 Abu Dhabi	20 San'a

Map countries: Kazakhstan · Uzbekistan · Kyrgyzstan · Turkmenistan · Tajikistan · Turkey · Afghanistan · Lebanon · Syria · Iran · Israel · Iraq · Kuwait · Pakistan · Jordan · Bahrain · Saudi Arabia · Qatar · United Arab Emirates · Oman · Yemen

35

Siberia and the Far East

More than one-fifth of the world's entire population lives in China. Although the crowded cities are growing, most people still live in villages. China is a Communist country and until recently farms and industries were run by the government. The cold lands of Siberia, which are part of Russia, lie to the north of China. Coal mining and drilling for oil and gas are important industries here. In Japan, most people work in factories, shops, and offices. Many of the factories produce high-tech electronic equipment.

◆ **LOOK AT THE BIG MAP.**
Can you find…
• a two-humped camel?
• the Great Wall of China?
• Tibetan religious objects?
• Hong Kong?
• the Yellow River?

Tibet
Tibet is famous for the Buddhist monks who play an important part in the traditional way of life. The religious leader, the Dalai Lama, also used to be the political leader. China took over Tibet in 1951. In 1959 China forced the Dalai Lama to live in exile (outside the country).

THE COUNTRIES OF THE FAR EAST
◆ Find the capital cities of each country.
1 Ulan Bator   5 Tokyo
2 Beijing   6 Taipei
3 Pyongyang   7 Macau
4 Seoul

The climate of Central Asia ranges from bitterly cold in the far north to hot and wet in the far south. Much of Siberia is cold, treeless tundra. Further south, in China, there are large deserts – the Gobi and the Takla Makan. In the southwest are the Himalayan mountains and the world's highest mountain, Everest. The Yangtze River and the Yellow River flow across eastern China. The islands of Japan are mountainous and covered in dense forests. Earthquakes are a danger in this area.

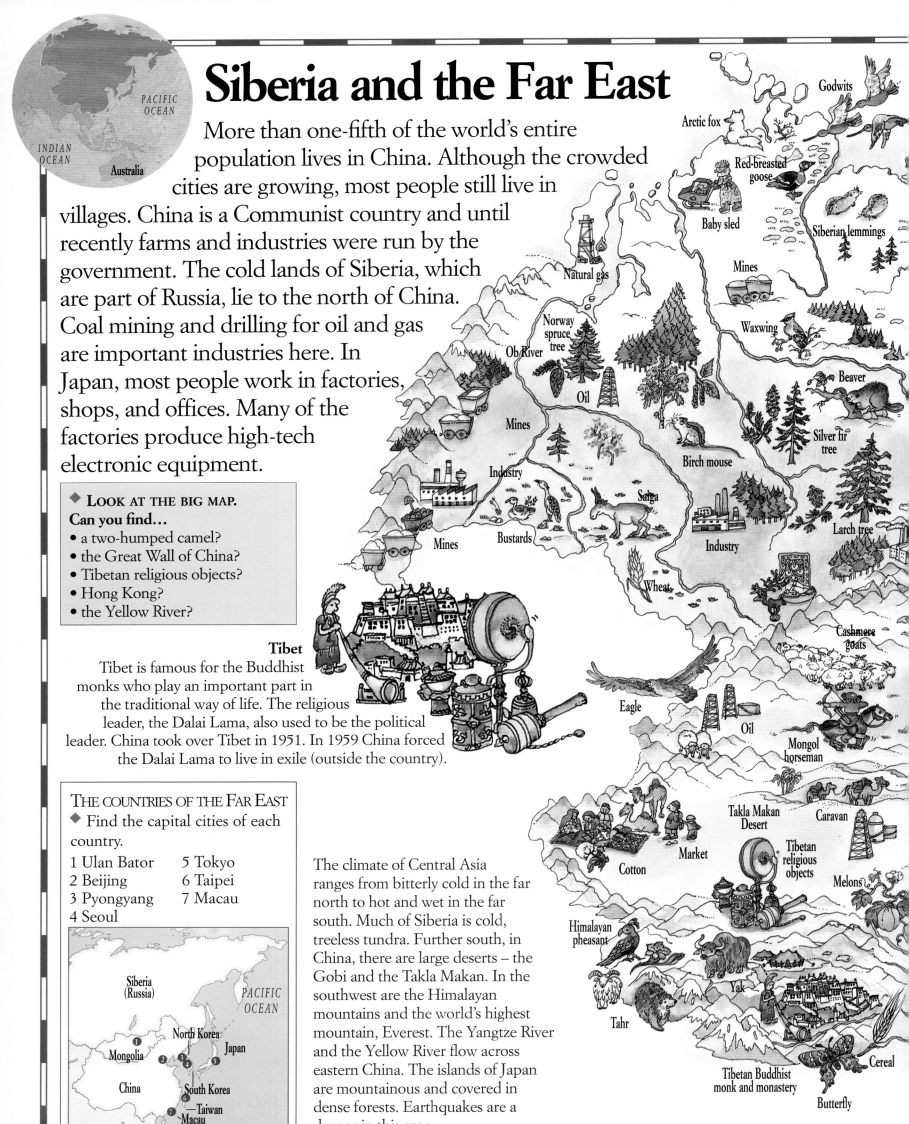

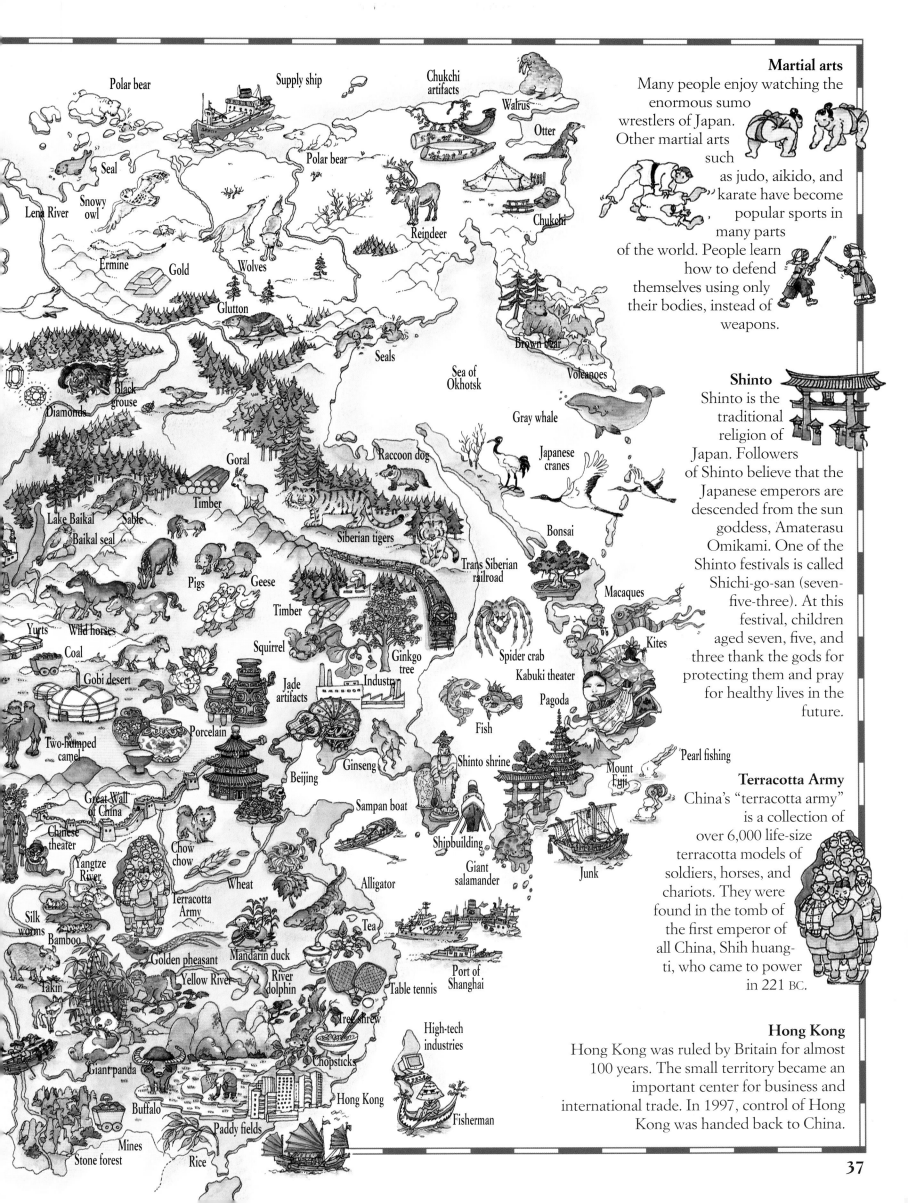

Polar bear
Supply ship
Chukchi artifacts
Walrus
Otter
Seal
Polar bear
Snowy owl
Lena River
Ermine
Gold
Wolves
Chukchi
Reindeer
Glutton
Brown bear
Seals
Sea of Okhotsk
Volcanoes
Black grouse
Gray whale
Diamonds
Goral
Raccoon dog
Japanese cranes
Timber
Bonsai
Lake Baikal
Sable
Siberian tigers
Baikal seal
Trans Siberian railroad
Pigs
Geese
Timber
Macaques
Squirrel
Kites
Yurts
Wild horses
Ginkgo tree
Spider crab
Coal
Industry
Kabuki theater
Gobi desert
Jade artifacts
Pagoda
Two-humped camel
Porcelain
Fish
Beijing
Ginseng
Shinto shrine
Mount Fuji
Great Wall of China
Sampan boat
Pearl fishing
Chinese theater
Chow chow
Shipbuilding
Yangtze River
Wheat
Giant salamander
Junk
Silk worms
Terracotta Army
Alligator
Bamboo
Tea
Golden pheasant
Mandarin duck
Yellow River
River dolphin
Table tennis
Port of Shanghai
Takin
Tree shrew
High-tech industries
Giant panda
Chopsticks
Buffalo
Hong Kong
Mines
Paddy fields
Fisherman
Stone forest
Rice

Martial arts

Many people enjoy watching the enormous sumo wrestlers of Japan. Other martial arts such as judo, aikido, and karate have become popular sports in many parts of the world. People learn how to defend themselves using only their bodies, instead of weapons.

Shinto

Shinto is the traditional religion of Japan. Followers of Shinto believe that the Japanese emperors are descended from the sun goddess, Amaterasu Omikami. One of the Shinto festivals is called Shichi-go-san (seven-five-three). At this festival, children aged seven, five, and three thank the gods for protecting them and pray for healthy lives in the future.

Terracotta Army

China's "terracotta army" is a collection of over 6,000 life-size terracotta models of soldiers, horses, and chariots. They were found in the tomb of the first emperor of all China, Shih huang-ti, who came to power in 221 BC.

Hong Kong

Hong Kong was ruled by Britain for almost 100 years. The small territory became an important center for business and international trade. In 1997, control of Hong Kong was handed back to China.

37

Growing rice
Rice is the most important crop grown in South Asia. It needs lots of water to grow, so before the seeds are planted, the fields are flooded. Water buffalo are used to churn up the mud. These flooded fields are called paddies.

Asia

PACIFIC OCEAN

INDIAN OCEAN

Australia

Markhor

Snow leopard

Ladakh jewellery

Shepherd

Dates

Carpet

Teapot

Saffron

Wheat

Asiatic black bear

Yak

Barheaded geese

Sherpa

Mount Everest

Bhutan masks

Red panda

Rubies

Camels

Snake charmer

Barley

Corn

Butterfly

Tiger

Antelope

Gerbil

Taj Mahal

Rhinoceros

Gavial

Golden lemur

Indus River

Green turtles

Lion

Sugarcane

Calcutta

Ganges River

Monk

Ganesh

Hornbill

Tiger

Sugarcane

Long-tailed porcupine

Rangoon

Eel

Religions
The people of South Asia follow many different religions. Buddhism, Hinduism, Islam, Sikhism, and Christianity are the main ones.

Cotton

Hindu festival

Sorghum

Bay of Bengal

Dragonfish

River trade

Painted stork

Spices

Shiva

Sitar

Siamese fighting fish

Palm squirrel

Indian dancer

Logging
Many forests in South Asia have been cut down. Logging is an important way for poor countries to earn money, but it has destroyed habitats and traditional ways of life. In Indonesia, forest fires have caused severe air pollution.

Hindu temple

Sloth bear

Reclining Buddha

Coconuts

Tin mines

Hammerhead shark

Sri Lanka

Porcupine fish

Dhows

Fishermen

Barracuda

Sumatran rhinoceroses

Grey whale

Scorpion fish

THE COUNTRIES OF SOUTH ASIA
◆ Match the names with the numbers on the map to find the capital cities of each country.

Nepal
Bhutan
India
Myanmar
Laos
Vietnam
Bangladesh
Thailand
Cambodia
Philippines
PACIFIC OCEAN
Sri Lanka
Maldives
Malaysia
Brunei
Singapore
Indonesia

1 New Delhi	9 Hanoi
2 Kathmandu	10 Manila
3 Thimphu	11 Kuala Lumpur
4 Dhaka	12 Bandar Seri Begawan
5 Rangoon	13 Singapore
6 Bangkok	14 Jakarta
7 Phnom Penh	15 Colombo
8 Vientiane	

Rare animals
Some of the world's rarest animals live in South Asia. These include the rhinos of Sumatra and Java, the orangutan, the sun bear, and the tiger.

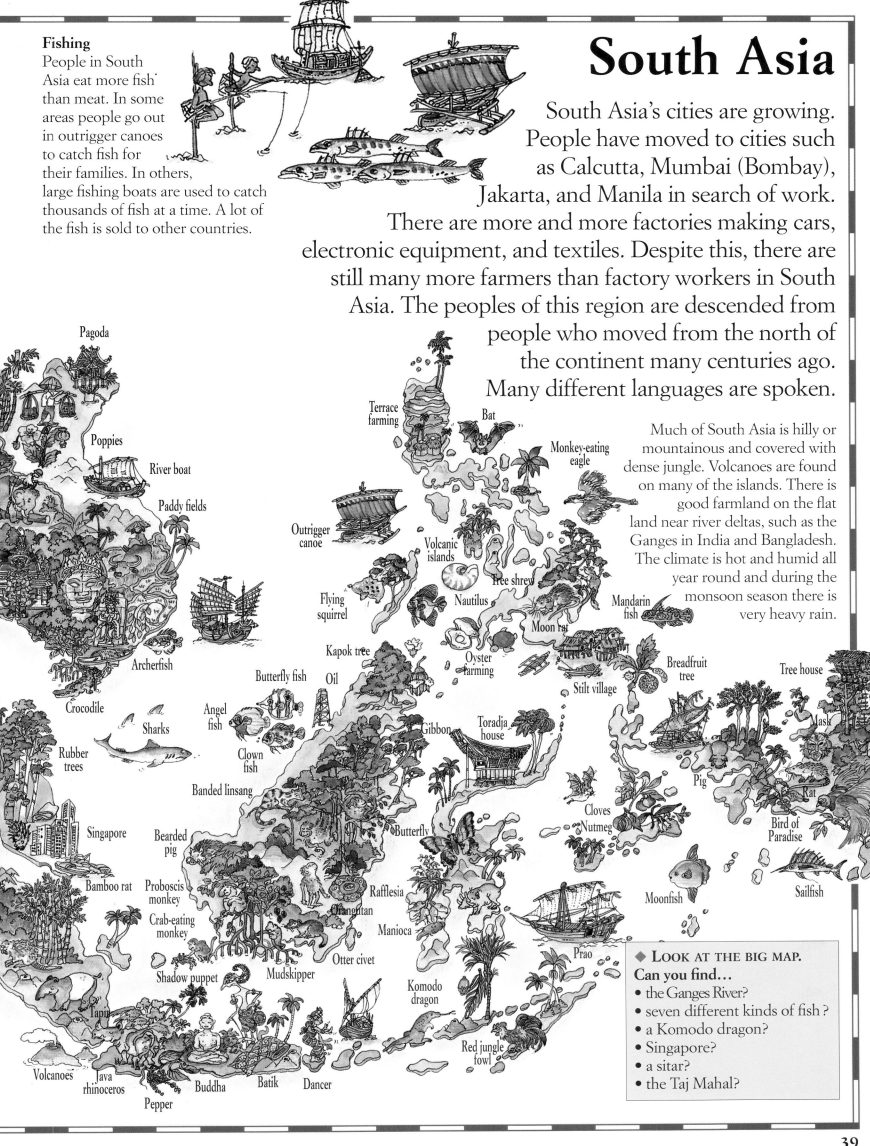

Fishing
People in South Asia eat more fish than meat. In some areas people go out in outrigger canoes to catch fish for their families. In others, large fishing boats are used to catch thousands of fish at a time. A lot of the fish is sold to other countries.

South Asia

South Asia's cities are growing. People have moved to cities such as Calcutta, Mumbai (Bombay), Jakarta, and Manila in search of work. There are more and more factories making cars, electronic equipment, and textiles. Despite this, there are still many more farmers than factory workers in South Asia. The peoples of this region are descended from people who moved from the north of the continent many centuries ago. Many different languages are spoken.

Much of South Asia is hilly or mountainous and covered with dense jungle. Volcanoes are found on many of the islands. There is good farmland on the flat land near river deltas, such as the Ganges in India and Bangladesh. The climate is hot and humid all year round and during the monsoon season there is very heavy rain.

Pagoda
Poppies
River boat
Paddy fields
Terrace farming
Bat
Monkey-eating eagle
Outrigger canoe
Volcanic islands
Flying squirrel
Nautilus
Tree shrew
Moon rat
Mandarin fish
Archerfish
Butterfly fish
Oil
Kapok tree
Oyster farming
Breadfruit tree
Tree house
Stilt village
Crocodile
Angel fish
Sharks
Clown fish
Gibbon
Toradja house
Mask
Rubber trees
Banded linsang
Pig
Rat
Singapore
Cloves
Nutmeg
Bird of Paradise
Bearded pig
Butterfly
Bamboo rat
Proboscis monkey
Rafflesia
Moonfish
Sailfish
Crab-eating monkey
Orangutan
Manioca
Otter civet
Prao
Shadow puppet
Mudskipper
Komodo dragon
Tapir
Volcanoes
Java rhinoceros
Buddha
Batik
Dancer
Red jungle fowl
Pepper

◆ **LOOK AT THE BIG MAP.**
Can you find…
- the Ganges River?
- seven different kinds of fish?
- a Komodo dragon?
- Singapore?
- a sitar?
- the Taj Mahal?

39

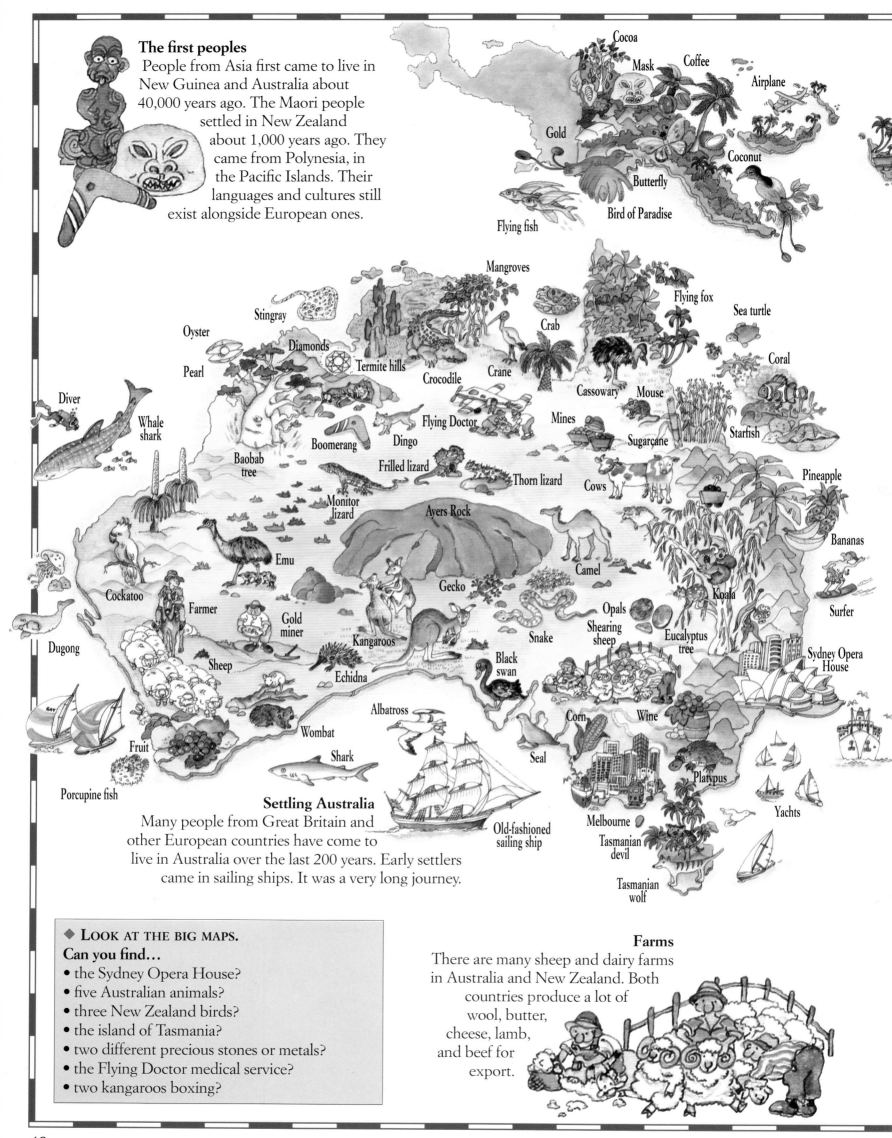

The first peoples

People from Asia first came to live in New Guinea and Australia about 40,000 years ago. The Maori people settled in New Zealand about 1,000 years ago. They came from Polynesia, in the Pacific Islands. Their languages and cultures still exist alongside European ones.

Cocoa
Mask
Coffee
Airplane
Gold
Coconut
Butterfly
Bird of Paradise
Flying fish

Mangroves
Stingray
Flying fox
Sea turtle
Oyster
Crab
Diamonds
Coral
Pearl
Termite hills
Crane
Crocodile
Cassowary
Mouse
Starfish
Diver
Mines
Sugarcane
Whale shark
Flying Doctor
Dingo
Boomerang
Pineapple
Baobab tree
Frilled lizard
Thorn lizard
Cows
Monitor lizard
Ayers Rock
Bananas
Emu
Camel
Koala
Cockatoo
Gecko
Surfer
Farmer
Camel
Opals
Dugong
Gold miner
Kangaroos
Snake
Shearing sheep
Eucalyptus tree
Sydney Opera House
Sheep
Echidna
Black swan
Wombat
Corn
Wine
Albatross
Fruit
Seal
Shark
Platypus
Porcupine fish
Yachts
Melbourne
Settling Australia
Old-fashioned sailing ship
Tasmanian devil
Tasmanian wolf

Many people from Great Britain and other European countries have come to live in Australia over the last 200 years. Early settlers came in sailing ships. It was a very long journey.

◆ **LOOK AT THE BIG MAPS.**

Can you find…
• the Sydney Opera House?
• five Australian animals?
• three New Zealand birds?
• the island of Tasmania?
• two different precious stones or metals?
• the Flying Doctor medical service?
• two kangaroos boxing?

Farms

There are many sheep and dairy farms in Australia and New Zealand. Both countries produce a lot of wool, butter, cheese, lamb, and beef for export.

Australasia

Most people in Australia and New Zealand live in towns and cities. There are also many farms, and agriculture is important for both countries. The majority of people speak English. There are many immigrants from all over the world. Papua New Guinea is the eastern half of the island of New Guinea. Many Papuans live in traditional ways in country villages, just as their ancestors have done for thousands of years.

Asia

PACIFIC OCEAN

INDIAN OCEAN

Great Barrier Reef

Great Barrier Reef is made of brightly colored coral. It is the largest reef in the world and stretches 1,250 miles down the east coast of Australia. The warm tropical waters near the reef are teeming with fish and other animals.

Special animals

There are some unique animals in Australia and New Zealand. Some, like kangaroos, koalas, and opossums have pouches on their tummies for carrying their babies. They are called marsupials. Others, like kiwis and emus, are birds that cannot fly.

Australasia is made up of the islands of Australia, New Zealand, and Papua New Guinea. Northern Australia and Papua have hot tropical climates. Australia has many large deserts. Southern Australia and New Zealand have cooler, temperate weather.

Cape Reinga
Citrus fruit
Gannets
Ocean liner
Kauri tree
Auckland City
Maori statue
Tuatara
Volcano
Cow
Vineyards
Apples
Kiwi
Rugby
Whale
Ferry boat
Weta
Dolphins
Takahe
Sheep
Christchurch Cathedral
Kea
Fishing boat
Rain forest
Kakapo
Sailing boat
Penguin

THE COUNTRIES OF AUSTRALASIA

◆ Find the capital cities of each country.

1 Canberra   2 Wellington   3 Port Moresby

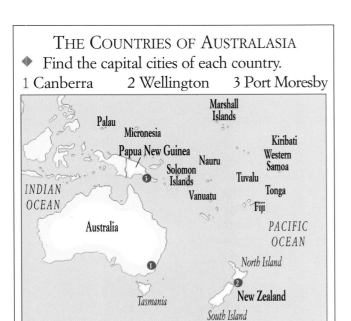

Palau
Marshall Islands
Micronesia
Papua New Guinea
Nauru
Kiribati
Western Samoa
Solomon Islands
Tuvalu
Vanuatu
Tonga
Fiji
INDIAN OCEAN
PACIFIC OCEAN
Australia
North Island
New Zealand
Tasmania
South Island

Tasmania is a part of Australia. New Zealand is divided into North Island and South Island.

Index

Bulgaria Sofia	**Romania** Bucharest	**Estonia** Tallinn	**Latvia** Riga	**Lithuania** Vilnius	**Belarus** Minsk	**Ukraine** Kiev
				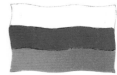		
Moldova Chisinau	**Georgia** Tbilisi	**Armenia** Yerevan	**Azerbaijan** Baku	**Russia** Moscow	**Turkey** Ankara	**Israel** Jerusalem

Lebanon Beirut	**Jordan** Amman	**Syria** Damascus	**Saudi Arabia** Riyadh	**Yemen** San'a	**Oman** Muscat	**United Arab Emirates** Abu Dhabi

Bahrain Manama	**Qatar** Doha	**Kuwait** Kuwait City	**Iraq** Baghdad	**Iran** Tehran	**Turkmenistan** Ashkhabat	**Afghanistan** Kabul

Uzbekistan Tashkent	**Kazakhstan** Astana	**Tajikistan** Dushanbe	**Kyrgyzstan** Bishkek	**Pakistan** Islamabad	**India** Delhi	**Nepal** Kathmandu

Bhutan Thimphu	**Bangladesh** Dhaka	**Sri Lanka** Colombo	**The Maldives** Malé	**China** Beijing	**Mongolia** Ulan Bator	**Japan** Tokyo

North Korea Pyongyang	**South Korea** Seoul	**Taiwan** Taipei	**Burma/Myanmar** Rangoon	**Thailand** Bangkok	**Laos** Vientiane	**Vietnam** Hanoi

Cambodia Phnom Penh	**Malaysia** Kuala Lumpur	**Singapore** Singapore	**Indonesia** Djakarta	**Brunei** Bandar Seri Begawan	**The Philippines** Manila	**Morocco** Rabat

Algeria Algiers	**Tunisia** Tunis	**Libya** Tripoli	**Egypt** Cairo	**Western Sahara** Al-Aioun	**Mauritania** Nouakchott	**Senegal** Dakar